ROCK & ROLL MURDERS

An Entrepreneur Finds Murder is No Business Solution

Based on a True Story By

Phillip B. Chute

Acknowledgment

For all the people who have contributed and made the writing and completion of this book possible, a special word of gratitude.

Disclaimer

Every effort has been made to fictionalize this book although the narration of some situations and representations by some characters may be based on underlying actual events. This book is based on a true story with many changes to protect the innocent and not to defame.

Prologue

Jackrabbit Trail, Badlands, May 29, 1991

On a smoggy spring day, the midday sun baked two California Highway Patrolmen in dark blue uniforms and a bearded dirt biker astride his Yamaha. They stood on a dirt road between the San Andreas barren earthquake faulted hills crisscrossed with biker's trails. The sergeant stood next to the still body of Eduardo Sanchez, a thirteen-year-old boy clad in t-shirt and gangware oversized shorts, lying on his back with three bullet wounds and powder burns tattooed on his forehead. An astonished look captured his small immature cold face.

A hundred yards down the road, rookie motorcycle police officer Ralph Hernandez cradled fourteen-year-old Manuel Rodriguez' head with one arm, holding a compress against the bullet wound in his back. He placed himself between the sun to shade the unconscious teen-ager. Blood covered the ground, seeping from his clothes. Eduardo was barely breathing, his color ashen, the color drained from his face. The rookie stopped blood seeping out of the punctured lung. He had a younger brother, much like the stranger. It had crossed in his mind when he first saw Eduardo on the road. Something bothered the officer. "Flies everywhere!" he screamed in frustration, as he ripped off his CHP helmet to slash at the buzzing insects circling them. Above, turkey vultures floated on wind currents in lazy circles.

A medivac chopper with Air Medical letters and a red cross on the fuselage barreled over a nearby hill, kicking up dust as it lowered and settled down. The sergeant waved the running paramedics on. "This kid's dead. Somebody executed him." The paramedic team rushed past them with their gear to Rookie Hernandez holding the other child.

"…taking him to Loma Linda Trauma?"

The paramedic nodded as his companion inserted the dextrose needle. "Jeez," he said, "the kid's veins are collapsing. I'm having a hell of a time getting the needle in." After a struggle, he said. "Thank, God! I got it!"

The older officer, a weathered ex-marine, always in control, watched the medical team stabilize the teenager. Then he strolled over to the jumpy bearded man smoking by the Yamaha. The Guns & Roses song *Live and Let Die* blared from the biker's portable radio! The radio disc jockey cheerfully interjected that they were listening to COLA Rock & Roll on the dial. "Say, fella, you mind turning the radio off? We need to talk." He looked away to watch the paramedics. "The other officer is pretty upset 'cause he has a brother a bit like the kid that was shot."

The biker turned the radio off. "Sorry about that, officer. I'm pretty scared just finding the boys," he paused, "Gang execution is a terrible thing, isn't it?"

The cool sergeant had his clipboard out, taking notes, then looked at his watch. "That's okay." He was very sincere and low key knowing both teenagers would be dead if the biker hadn't called. "We appreciate you calling us and hanging around. If only more people were good citizens like you."

The biker smiled, tossed his lit cigarette into the dirt. He could hardly wait to tell his buddies about the events. The officer gave him a hard look. "Sorry," he said, stamping out the butt.

The sergeant continued. "Could I see your driver's license, please? And your phone number." He hesitated, and then gave the pat answer to the crime question. He didn't want to give anything away that would come back to haunt him in court. "Sorry, I can't speculate about the crime." The biker shoved his California license and phone number to the sergeant. "Now please put the bike back in your truck and meet me at the Badlands Substation. Here's your license and my card. Ask for me so I can take your statement."

The big chopper lifted off with the wounded kid. The Woodland County Sheriff's patrol car arrived, piercing shimmering heat waves and leaving a cloud of dust that obscured the twisted road. A coroner's van followed with other patrol cars.

The rookie slowly moved to his fellow officer. He smiled thinly. "We're in luck. The kid...he's a strong one. He started mumbling something when the paramedics got him in the chopper...." The young officer still looked dazed; a rookie's emotional shock not yet hardened with the passage of time and exposure. He paused.

Impatiently, the sergeant took a deep breath. The rookie, meantime, with the image of the two boys still in his mind—finally remembered what the kid kept saying, "Domingo, Domingo. They owed Domingo twenty dollars."

The sergeant's sudden satisfying smile caused his face to wake up, the first emotion he'd shown all day. He put his arm around the rookie's shoulder, explaining his coolness at the murder scene. "You get kinda numb, like in 'Nam, when your buddies get killed...'that these things don't bother you so much." They moved to the sergeant's patrol car. "Let's turn this over to the sheriff, then we'll go to the station and clean up. We've got work to do." He turned his head in disgust. "Jesus, a kid getting wasted for a lousy twenty bucks."

Sergeant Hernandez nodded, looking up into the sky as a shadow passed over him. He knew that evening he would be trying to hide the facts from his wife and the blood wouldn't go away. It would be a miserable time...a miserable but exciting job. His mind wandered back to Nam where another teen was killed. They had taken fire from a village and his patrol was running from hooch to hooch looking for the Viet Cong. He stepped into one where a young girl, about the same age as the kids on the ground, was standing up against a wall, white-faced, scared, and trembling. Something about her eyes wasn't right, though. During the moment he paused, she raised a revolver from her skirt and pulled the trigger. It hit an empty chamber. The hammer rose again as he quickly fired a burst from the AR 15 on full auto. *That was war, justifiable killing, not like today*, he thought, but the memory kept returning time and time again and he was unable to erase her dark intense eyes from his mind.

The dozen turkey buzzards returned, their ugly red heads and necks crowning huge black and brown bodies, patiently waiting for the evidence team and photographer to finish their tasks in the yellow taped crime perimeter. They circled overhead until their lunch left in the coroner's van.

1

The Inn, January 1970

Alice Barro was five years old when the family made the nightmare trip from Missouri. The station wagon was loaded and racked with poor folks' household goods. She and her older sister, Ellie, crammed into the front seat between her father and mother. For endless fitful hours they drove from the plains to the Mojave Desert, then finally chugged past the Vasquez rocks which they recognized from old cowboy movies. The old Ford, wheezing and smoking, climbed the final mountain pass separating the San Gabriel Mountains from the San Bernardino Range. With a whoop and a holler, the exhausted passengers descended through the El Cajon Pass to the railroad hub of San Bernardino.

Alice remembered her mother; unhappy with father's poor earnings at local gas station and abandoned her and Ellie the next year to go off with a musician to San Francisco. She was never heard of again. Her mother blamed everything on father, repeating, "*We left poverty in* Missouri *to find more poverty in San Bernardino.*"

One day, through a Catholic Church organization, Alice and Ellie were offered an opportunity for adoption with different local families. She became Alice Knight, lived in a small trailer park in Bloomington with a childless middle-aged couple in nearby Rialto; they offered her opportunity to be a proper young lady. Catholic religion and parochial school structured her life where there had been none before. Her real father visited on Sunday afternoons. He took her to the mountain villages where they'd drink sodas and share ice cream. Alice never saw the rooming house where he lived. A few years later, he died when a failed hydraulic lift crushed him at work.

Alice then found peace with the loving stability offered by the Knights but her poverty continued. Frozen shredded fish sticks on Fridays, tough beef round steak on Saturdays with meat loaf and macaroni in between. Old clothes were washed and sewn until the seams wore out. Her sister, living nearby, coughed all the time from smog and asthma.

Alice enrolled in a nursing program which began after high school. She made $2.65 an hour. Later that year, she was introduced at a church function to Raymond, sixteen years her senior. He was five foot eight, poorly dressed, but reported to have his own business…the equivalent of being rich by her mother who insisted that Alice date him. "But Mom," Alice protested, tossing her shoulder-length black hair back, gray eyes protesting from ruddy complexion, "I'm not interested in old men. I have boys making eyes at me all the time. Besides, I hate how he dresses."

"You're a beautiful girl and can have your pick of men," Said her gray-haired mother. "You can have freedom, travel, and enjoy life. He told me he was only eight years older then you. Besides, you can twist him around your finger later on." Alice nodded obediently and several months later the arrangements were made.

The first date was in the mobile home. Alice wore a long chiffon skirt and a ruffled blouse. Her mother served tea and biscuits. Raymond wore his best chinos with a new shiny brown polyester long-sleeved cuff linked shirt which made him sweat. He brought chocolates for the mother and a set of Nancy Drew mystery novels and flowers for Alice. The brief encounter was stiff. When the meeting finally ended, Alice ran to her room crying.

Afterward, Alice dated local boys which reinforced her Mother's theory that Rialto is not Beverly Hills, and that none of the locals had a future. A year later she reluctantly let her mother make another date with Raymond, but this time at a restaurant. She appeared older then her true age because of her height and strong character.

Ruben's was the classiest watering hole in town. The restaurant offered high-backed plush naugahyde seating and privacy. Even when busy, it accommodated many a deal or proposition over an expensive meal saturated with alcohol. A wall separated the dining room from the wet bar. Two wall-mounted televisions over the bar exhibited sporting events and evening news to an almost empty room. Light chatter drifted from the restaurant side to the front reception room.

When Raymond McDade entered the restaurant, he looked for Alice in the crowded waiting area. "Looking for a tall lady?" the hostess asked, looking up from the reservation pad. He nodded. Raymond wore a navy blue polyester suit with a bright flowered tie, penny loafers, and a white shirt with gold-plated crown-emblem cufflinks. He was out of place among the few smartly dressed businessmen. Ray seemed older than his thirty-six years. He had only a monkish rim of red hair over his ears, capping his pale, reddish Irish complexion. His muscles lacked tone and looked soft, although he was not overweight for his frame. He had similar soft facial features around his small eyes, nose and mouth. Tonight he was all business; anxious for a mate. He had been worried about being stood up. *Maybe she's not here; a different girl. I should have stayed at the station to catch up on my work*, he thought. But he knew there was no real substitute for being lonely. The hostess pointed out Alice as she walked in. Alice, twenty years old, raven black hair, soft olive colored skin suggestive of Mediterranean ancestors with strong and attractive facial features, was in a plush chair sipping a coke in the far corner. She caught Raymond's eye, and waved to him.

"Hello Alice, you're looking lovely tonight." He strode to her and led her to the hostess to be seated. With her high heels she was taller then Ray, cutting a fine figure in her tight-fitting designer jeans.

She's grown up, he thought. *I'll bet she's great in bed.* They sat down smiling. "Glad to see you again, Alice."

"Likewise, Ray.

"You look great, honey. I thought you'd be in the bar."

"Yeah, but I'm barely old enough to drink yet." She knew she'd need a real drink before long with Raymond.

The waitress approached and Ray ordered a martini. "Dry or regular?" she asked.

"Dry okay."

"Shaken, not stirred?" Alice asked with a smile, and ordered another coke. A minute later the waitress delivered the drink and Raymond sipped, with his face souring from the unfamiliar ginny taste. Alice looked at her drink, not him. "Are you James Bond tonight?"

"No. Just Raymond McDade, the radio guy." He put on his best smile for her.

"You're too old to be a disc jockey," she said. And I guess you don't dress like James Bond." Now she studied him, including his argyle socks. She was curious about his business. *This guy is no Charles Atlas,* she thought, *and he dresses like a clown, but maybe he has something going for him besides his age. After all, Mom always says to marry money and an older man. The young high school hunks never have anything going for them except their looks and an empty wallet. Her mother should know; they'd lived in poverty.*

"You're young enough to be my secretary but look old enough to have a drink. Your mother said you were working as a nurse. You're too nice to be emptying bedpans." He looked her over slowly, from top to bottom.

Alice ran her fingers through her long hair, arching her chest forward. Greed ran through her mind. *Maybe he was telling the truth*, she thought. "Actually, I'm twenty-one now, and I need a good job. You work in a radio station?"

"I own three of them," he lied because he only had one. Now, with a grin on his face, he watches her like a fish on a hook. "Waitress, I'd like another drink and one for the lady, please."

"Coke for the lady and another Martini?"

"I changed my mind," Ray said, "Perhaps a Tom Collins for both of us, okay?" Alice nodded and the waitress left.

"Now, you're not putting me on about owning three radio stations?" He nodded his head to confirm the lie. She continued talking before he could say anything. "Here, let me show you a trick I learned as a kid." She took the cherry out of her drink, plucked the stem off with her teeth, placing the stem into her mouth and with her tongue worked mysterious convolutions inside her cheek for a long minute. Suddenly Alice spit out the stem on her napkin. She blushed, picked up the neatly knotted stem with her long red nails. "Viola!" she exclaimed, exhibiting the prize, placing it in front of Ray.

"Now," she challenged, "what can you do?"

Ray took a wad of bills out of his trouser pocket, placed it carefully on the bar in front of him. He snapped the thick rubber band surrounding the lot. "That's what I can do, lady."

Alice stared at the wad, thinking. *It could be a year's salary at the hospital.* She looked him up and down again, comparing his attire with his wealth. "Naw, it's an Oakie bankroll. Just a wad of ones," she said.

Raymond slid the money over to her. "See for yourself. There's about ten grand there." Alice leafed through the roll, all hundred-dollar bills with the smallest bills on the outside of the fold. She was getting religion. "Well, now I like you a lot." She pushed the wad back to him. "Let's have dinner."

They ordered prime rib.

"This is the greatest steak I ever had," Alice said after cleaning her plate, and over another Tom Collins.

"I'm glad you like it. My family grew up near Chicago and on Saturdays they would go to the outside market in East Chicago near Faneuil Hall for meat. Sometimes it was old and moldy. Italian shopkeepers hung chickens upside down during Easter and there was sawdust on the floor." He paused, "and there was always fresh fish for Fridays which we'd keep on ice. We never had steak, especially a good steak like this."

"It's tough being Catholic," she said. We have fish sticks on Fridays. God knows what they're made of...but I can't complain, being adopted and all."

"Really?" Ray leaned over the table, "I was adopted, too. My mother never married my father and when they finally married years later, he legally adopted me."

They drank a toast to being adopted and then left. Ray didn't leave a tip.

Alice noticed. "You forgot to leave a tip."

"I never tip. They're paid a salary for their work." Ray said, ignoring Alice's look.

Alice fished in her purse and dropped some dollar bills on the table. As they walked out Alice wondered how anybody could be so cheap. Her disgust slowly disappeared however, as she thought of all the money available to spend on her.

"Nice meeting you, Ray," Alice said in parting. "Let's meet again."

"I have a better idea. Follow me to the radio station and I'll show you the business." She agreed and they left.

Alice parked her small Datsun compact and strode over to Ray's new Chevy sedan at the Inn parking lot. They went to the corner of the historic building a block away.

"Your car has dealer plates?" Alice said, "I thought you were in the radio business."

"I hate to pay taxes so I trade advertising time for merchandise." He smiled to himself. "It's not bad for the dealer because he'll sell it as an executive car a year later and only lose a couple of hundred on it. The stupid people think they're getting a good deal on a new car because it was never sold."

They arrived at the Inn Rotunda. "You're a pretty smart guy, Ray," Alice said as he unlocked the huge doors. She stared at the beautiful wide spiral staircase with the huge fountain at its base. National crests in bright colors adorned the walkway above the columns above each level. They entered on a ground floor with another floor below and five above. Arched entrances were set back from the stairs on seven different levels. Moonlight poured through the open top, casting mysterious shadows everywhere. Alice clutched his hand. "This is amazing! I've never been here before. Is your business here someplace?"

"Right here, on the second floor." They went around the stairs where light shined through the stained glass windows of his office. "I live here, too, upstairs in a tiny studio apartment."

"Sounds like you're married to the business. Must keep you pretty busy!" Suddenly, she stopped. "How many times have you been married? Do you pay alimony?" She pulled at his arm to turn him around to face her. "Are you married now?"

Raymond placed his hands on her broad shoulders. "I'm divorced, but you're right. I am married to the business. It was losing money when I bought it, and I worked full-time at another station until I made it work and bought out my financial partner."

Alice was still concerned with his relationships. "You don't pick up the bimbos on University Avenue for entertainment, do you? A guy could catch all kinds of diseases from those girls."

Raymond grinned. "I have girlfriends, but mostly, I just work here all the time. A radio station runs twenty-four hours a day; it never sleeps. If I were married now, it would be my mistress because it's so demanding," he laughed aloud. Light was shining through a glass door as Ray unlocked it. A wall of electronic equipment was visible in the back of the large control room. The Doors were pounding out *Light My Fire* through the studio. A young man carrying a textbook greeted them, "Hi, Boss."

"Hey, Jim, this is Alice." Jim nodded in response and returned to his desk by the electronic panel. Ray turned to Alice who was staring at the panel lights and reel-to-reel tape drives slowly turning. "Jim's my night engineer; he makes sure we don't go dark."

"Dark?"

"No, honey," Ray chuckled. "Dark is when we lose transmitting power and switch on the backup system…or we could lose our Federal Communications Commission license. That's why you hear the music. Like I said, the station never sleeps."

Alice nodded without understanding, but now she smiled at him. She had never associated with smart people except the doctors at the hospital who were in a different world, with their degrees and big salaries. She felt she had stepped into a storybook castle and this guy controlled it. A quiver went down her spine. "You know, Ray, this is a beautiful business and you did it all yourself."

Ray grasped her hand. "I just moved the business last month and need a salesman and a secretary-receptionist. I can pay you twice what you make as a nurses aide. Are you up for it? The secretary job, I mean?"

"Wow…uh…yeah. I don't take shorthand but I need a good job and love 'Rock and Roll.' It sure beats dumping bed pans." This is a wonderful business. I could tell my Mom and sister that I listen to 'Rock and Roll' music for a living!" Alice looked around at all the equipment. The music and studio mesmerized her, leaving her lightheaded especially after the two drinks in the restaurant. "Where does the sound go from here?"

"A satellite dish on the roof of the Inn sends the signal to a tower in the mountains which sends it everywhere," he explained, pulling her into a small room with a desk piled high with papers. A streetlight outside a leaded glass window cast a mosaic of colored light on the inside wall. It disappeared as Ray switched on a light, took an unopened bottle of brandy and plastic cups from a desk drawer, then poured two drinks.

Alice looked around at the piles of papers stacked on the floor, on the shelves behind the desk and on a sofa with a flower pattern that went out of style fifty years ago. The room was in absolute contrast to the neat, orderly humming equipment room.

Raymond closed the door, handing her a drink. "Here's to us and COLA," he continued. "Let's toast to 31,000 watts of power and everybody between Los Angeles and the Inland Empire at 100 on the FM dial!" They drank the brandy straight up. Ray placed his hands on her hips. He kissed her, tasting lipstick and cheap brandy. She tried to relax as his hands moved up from her waist; then she pulled away, closing her eyes as she swallowed the remaining brandy.

"A lady never jumps into bed on a first date!" she said with a coy smile. "Gosh, Ray, slow down." Suddenly she stood, realizing she'd gone too far with the stranger. "I've got to get home." She pushed him away.

Ray reached for her once again, but was rebuffed. "Okay, Lady. I guess I went too fast." His face was red with frustration. Alice opened the door to escape.

Leaving the office after smoothing out her clothes, she stumbled over papers on the floor. Her speech was slurred. "Thanks for the wonderful time, Raymond." She pushed her long hair away from her face as she lurched out the doorway. "I'd love to start work next week as you promised. Nurse's aides don't make any money, you know."

They walked down the stairs together, Alice stumbling. At the bottom Raymond generously peeled a hundred dollar bill off his roll. "Here you go.

It's a payroll cash advance to make sure you show up for work. Hope you get home okay."

Alice looked at the bill which was more than a weeks pay at the hospital. "Thanks, Ray. Thanks a lot."

Ray looked at her hungrily, contemplating her figure, completely sober while always in control. "You'll never regret working for me," he promised. The cold air outside refreshing them as they walked to her car. Alice recovered enough to walk straight.

Ray continued, "Maybe you can start earlier so I can interview for a salesman. It won't look right for me to have this big business without a secretary, would it? Can you start in two days?"

Alice soured, "I'll try, but the hospital usually requires a week or two or they don't give a good reference." She paused, her steel gray eyes looking into his brown eyes, liking his sincerity. He smiled and they kissed goodbye. Alice headed toward her car, and then looked back at Ray before driving away. He appeared a comic character, the balding man in his terrible suit. *Maybe this guy was only half a man compared to the macho guys in construction*, she thought to herself. *Half a rich man.*

Alice, who was adopted by strangers, had met Raymond who was adopted by his own father, would meet Domingo Malichera, who was also adopted by relatives. Two murders and two attempted murders would result from this fateful alchemy.

2

Animal Farm

Animal control officer Terry Garcia stepped out of his truck, checked the address on his clipboard and then surveyed the old residential neighborhood. It's like an Oakie neighborhood, he thought. *The more beat-up cars you park on your front lawn, the richer you are.* Desert heat struck him as though he'd opened an oven door. Wiping sweat off his brow he proceeded down the walkway, past unmowed high weeds to the front door. A tall, thin young man, about twenty-five, wearing cowboy boots, a Coors T-shirt and jeans, cracked open the door. Clattering animal and bird noises rushed out the door along with strong, unpleasant smells. The officer asked, "Do you live here?"

"What can I do for you, buddy?" said Mitch.

"We received a complaint that somebody was keeping dangerous animals or poisonous snakes at this address." A heavy thump accompanied by a loud hiss from inside startled Garcia who quickly regained his composure, "Would that be you? I need to look inside, please. Or I will get a warrant," he added.

Mitch saw the officer was going to enter one way or the other. "Okay, sure, come in but watch your step. I have lots of pets." He opened the door to dozens of animal cages occupied by big banded iguana lizards, exotic colorful Amazonian birds, garter snakes, various rodents, white Dutch rabbits, and a brown hen chicken. A noisy bright green parrot squawked in the background.

"This place is a zoo, mister. What's your full name"

"Mitchell Gallo. Now, sir…there's nothing illegal about having pets, is there?"

"There can be if they're endangered species, dangerous, or poisonous." Officer Garcia paused. "Or just a public nuisance." He jotted down the name on a clipboard and carefully stepped, looking at the creatures. Seeds, feed, straw bits, fast food containers, beer cans, littered the floor. "Why don't you keep them outside, Mr. Gallo?"

"They'd fry in the heat. I lost a lot that way."

"You're either crazy or in the pet business. We had a call last week on a lady whose husband died. He lived in the house next door with seventy-five cats. We took them all away. Imagine living with seventy-five cats." He grinned, remembering the cat round-up and herding exercise. "Where do you get these animals?"

"Mostly from Mexico. I get them for friends," he lied.

"Well, you're in trouble if any of them are dangerous." Garcia studied a tangle of striped garter snakes knotted in a ball in one cage, then moved to the turtles in a child's wading pool. "I'm not an expert on turtles, but if any of these are desert tortoises, you have a big problem."

"These are water turtles, not desert. See here." Mitch dug through a pile of books and magazines in a corner next to the television. Leafing through 'Turtles of the Universe,' he pointed to a green turtle identical to the one in the pool. "Here, look at this," thrusting the book at Garcia. They were interrupted by a heavy bumping noise coming from a closed door off a short hallway. "What's down there, Sir?"

"Just my rosy boa; he lives in the bedroom. I have to keep him separate from my other…pets." He walked to the door with Garcia cautiously following, opened the door slowly. "Poor Oscar, he fell off the dresser!" Mitch said. "I left him on the dresser this morning; he must have bruised himself when he fell. Snakes are all muscle, you know. He's sure mad now." A huge snake, squirming in pain, raised its head to hiss at his master.

Garcia peered over Mitch's shoulder, wagged his head in awe. "Wow! I've never seen a Rosie that big, even at the zoo. Why didn't you name her Rosie? It lives in your bedroom all the time?"

"I know what you're thinking. Oscar's a boy and only eats once a month. I was going to feed him today but not with him so mad."

Garcia grinned. "Aren't you afraid it'll swallow your arm," he looks down at Mitch's crotch, "or something while you're sleeping?"

Mitch grinned in return. "See that little baseball bat by the bed? Never used it, yet."

"Well, Sir, I know you must like animals a lot, but this is too much. You have either a business or a public nuisance…maybe both. I suggest you thin out the collection considerably."

"Would you like a nice cool beer or Coke to cool off? The swamp cooler helps here but not enough."

"Well, I'm not supposed to--maybe a Coke." He followed Mitch to the kitchen. Country-Western music was playing on a radio. Dolly Parton sounded great. Looking through the kitchen window he saw a huge heavy wire cage completely enclosed both top and sides and dominating the yard.

"What's that? An aviary?"

"Naw, that's Tiger's place. I haven't had time to take it down."

"Tiger? As in cat?"

I used to have a leopard named Tiger. A friend had a wild animal act in a nightclub on Van Buren Avenue." Mitch opened the refrigerator, took two cokes out, and handed Garcia one. "One day a drunken customer decided to pull Tiger's whiskers to show his girlfriend he wasn't afraid of him…well, he pulled, and the cat swatted him on the side of the head."

"Did he live?"

Sure, just missing an ear. The cat ate it, so they couldn't sew it back on. At any rate, the trainer knew the act was over and let me keep the cat." Mitch sat across the table from Garcia. "Man, I've got to know who called you. The neighbors close by all keep dogs and horses."

"Maybe somebody who doesn't like you? Have any enemies?"

Mitch jumped up almost knocking over his chair. "My ex. That bitch! She'd do anything to get me!!"

Garcia diverted his attention… "I got to write up a report giving you ten days to get rid of the zoo and clean up. I'll be back then. If this is your business, I suggest another line of work." He gave Mitch his business card on his way to the front door.

"When you come back you can see me feed Oscar. He'll really be hungry then."

The phone rang as the door closed. A gruff voice came over the line. "You sell parrots?"

"Sure, I have a lovely young bird right here now!"

"Well, my wife wants somebody to talk to. She says they talk a lot. Is it friendly?"

Mitch reached for a pencil and paper. "Buddy, I've got the friendliest parrot in Fontana. I can even deliver it today for only $250." Gruff man agreed and Mitch hung up, walking over to the green screeching parrot. "Got a new home for you, Talker and Squawker. It'll sure be quiet after you leave."

Mitch left, placing the cage on the front seat of the pick-up where the parrot could talk to him. The starter screeched…causing the bird to screech in return, then the ten-year-old Ford rattled out of the driveway.

Mitch was hungry but tired of fast food. He headed for The Office Café off the freeway in Colton, where he could always get a big cheap breakfast. His passenger squawked to him all the way. Country Western music played on the truck radio until he parked outside the small restaurant located in an office complex. The sun reflected off STAGE COACH RADIO in Gold letters mounted high across the building next door, visible from the freeway. Credence Clearwater Revival was still singing *Down on the Corner* inside the little restaurant.

He entered the poorly lit place and sat at the counter, not noticing Alice at a small table by the wall. "Where's all the customers, Mack?" He smiled at the cook.

"They all work for a living. It's ten-thirty in the morning, you know."

"Well, I hope it's not too late for Salisbury steak and eggs. I'm working too…

delivering a parrot to a Kaiser steel worker in Fontana whose wife wants a parrot." He laughed out loud. "That thing'll drive her nuts!"

"They get paid real good, those union steel workers. Coffee?" The waiter turned away and returned with an earthenware mug and pot. He poured thick black stuff before disappearing into the back kitchen to prepare the order.

Ray sipped on his coffee for five minutes before the waiter reappeared with the hamburger steak, gravy, and hash browns. Four pieces of toast followed. Mitch's sight adjusted to the dark room and he noticed Alice and waved, "Howdy."

Alice sometimes visited the hole-in-the-wall place where the cook served good food at a reasonable price when tired of oatmeal at home or sandwiches and coffee at the Woodland General Hospital cafeteria. "What do you do besides delivering parrots?" She asked.

"Had an animal farm but now I need a job 'cause the frigging government's closing me down."

Alice liked the simple cowboy and said, "I'm leaving for a better job next week. Gave notice at the hospital but have to stay longer because my supervisor needs a break to find a replacement. If she was a jerk, I'd leave today."

Mitch smiled at her. "You could work for me any day, but I don't have a job now." Then as an afterthought, "I'm Mitch Gallo." He bounced over to shake her hand, noting how straight she sat in her starched scrubs. There was an aura of strength and independence about her which attracted him.

"You know, cowboy, you're a nice guy. I'd bet you could sell anything." She fished through her purse, wrote a name and number on a napkin, placing it in front of Mitch.

Mitch reached out and grabbed it, blushing. "Wow! You're giving me your name and number!"

Alice laughed at his embarrassment, noting how inexperienced he was with women. "No, cowboy, I'm not propositioning you. This guy, Ray, is looking for a salesman. If you cleaned up, I'd bet he'd hire you. You sure have a great tan...could pass for James Caan."

"I'm part Cherokee. I don't sell insurance or phones. I need a job to start a new life.... just got divorced last year." He paused. "I need to move now because the animal control people don't like the farm. I think my ex set me up. Still need to complete the property settlement with her even though I don't have nothing."

Alice smiled at the tall naive cowboy with the tan and black hair under the big hat. His boots made him taller than his six feet... "This job might be good for you because the guy has tons of money and needs to sell ads for the radio station COLA." She grinned. "I'm starting there next week."

Mitch broke into a smile. "Thanks, lady. Maybe I'll see you there. I haven't had much to do with females since I split."

Alice finished her coffee, left her table, and then stood in the door as Mitch was wiping his plate clean with toast. "Call him right away and say Alice sent you. Good luck."

"I'll try. Thanks a lot." Mitch left thinking about the tall dark-haired stranger. *She sure is nice to look at, and bold as brass too. Maybe I'll hit it off with her.*

He returned to the demanding noisy parrot jumping up and down in his cage on the front seat of the pick-up. Mitch and Talker made silly bird talk as he drove away. He never would have delivered the friendly bird if he had any premonition of the parrot's murder.

3

Radio Station At The Inn

Mitch entered the control room where Raymond stood at a table working on the guts of a large platform of electronic tubes, condensers and wires. A hole in the wall rack showed where one of the four banks of equipment was missing. Raymond wore a plaid short-sleeved shirt with chino pants. The Rolling Stones played *Honkey Tonk Women* in the background.

Mitch approached Ray, and said, "Hi, I'm looking for Raymond McDade."

Ray studied the young man wearing Levis, blue denim shirt with pearl pocket buttons, Remington Arms belt buckle gripping a Mexican hand-tooled leather belt, and fancy pointed boots. *What am I supposed to do with a cowboy?* he thought. "I'm Raymond. You Mitch Gallo?"

Mitch stuck out his hand. "Yeah, I'm your new salesman, Mitch Gallo."

Ray cracked a smile at the cowboy's boldness. "Well, let's talk about it first." Ray motioned for him to sit on a metal folding chair and disappeared into his unlit office. Ray reappeared from the cave and handed Mitch a stapled set of documents from the Broadcaster's Association. "Here, read this. Then we'll talk." Ray returned to the electronic unit, "Excuse me while I work on this. It went out last night and I had to switch on the back-up unit. If I can't find the right amplifier tube I'll have to call in my engineer."

Mitch briefly scanned the handout and then began talking while Ray was still working. "This is insurance company stuff. My buddy sells life insurance and has the same closing routines; they just change the words."

Ray looked up saying, "Well, now, tell me about it." He returned to testing components by plugging tubes into a large testing machine that had many plug-in sockets, dials and switches.

Mitch leafed through the ten pages of large-type literature. "...like the 'closing circle' and never taking a no answer. Hell, that's like romancing a girl and never taking no for an answer. Some of this is funny, though."

"What?" Ray's impatience showed in his voice.

"Closing deal number eight. The idea of giving the client a taste of the advertising like taking the puppy home for a weekend to try him out. That's like a girl letting you in her pants to get married."

Raymond gave Mitch an annoying look. "Maybe we're getting off course here. I'm talking about selling advertising to businesses and you're talking about girls. I need a guy who can close a deal, not chase skirts."

Mitch defensively explained, "Don't get me wrong. The canned pitch has its place…maybe on the telephone to get appointments. But in business you deal with the secretary before you meet the owner. Once past the secretary, they'll buy anything that helps the business." Mitch maintained eye-to-eye contact with Ray to show his sincerity. He wasn't sophisticated but could level with this nerd. "Show me your business, and I'll bring customers in. Besides, don't worry about me chasing girls. I got divorced last year, a nasty deal. It'll be a long time before I'll be a knight in shining armor again. This is strictly business for me."

The cowboy's boldness impressed Ray. "Let me tell you a bit about the business. I bought out my partner a year ago. He was the sales guy, the outside partner. When he left to buy his own station in Santa Barbara I managed the sales myself from inside. Then I moved the station to this new office. What do you think of the place?"

"It's beautiful. I love it here. It's so old, like being inside a castle. I used to explore the Inn when I was a kid."

Raymond smiled and opened up. "Good. You're right…back to the story. I need to build the business up again. I need somebody who isn't afraid to cold call businesses, especially the car dealers. I have house accounts and national accounts from agencies, but not near enough."

"What's that?"

"Build my own station with sound rooms, a real control room, and office space for a big business." He paused, concerned about the cowboy problem. "You seem to be dressed like the competition, the Country-Western Stage Coach people. Got everything but the string tie and ten-gallon hat."

Mitch needed the job badly, enough to convert his musical taste and faith. "I was their fan until today. I'll learn to like Rock and Roll again. What's the pay?"

"I'll pay 10% of the billing after collection. That's really a lot of money because the car dealerships pay big money to run their phony crap every weekend."

Mitch felt him caving. "If I take the job, how do I live till the money comes in?." He leaned forward, to pressure Ray, "What about a car allowance or expenses?"

Ray saw what he wanted in the cowboy; liked his originality and boldness. He sensed the guy would work out and that they connected. Ray softened and offered, "I'll pay you minimum wage until you can offset it with your commissions. That'll be enough to pay your expenses. Use the office phones for your calls. I'll cover mail costs and office supplies. If you survive the first month, you'll never regret working here."

Ray could see Mitch relaxing and smiled back. "I'll cut you a check at the end of next week for your first month. Call it an advance. I like your boldness, but you need to produce, work hard, and make those calls. Understand?." Mitch nodded and started to speak but Ray held up his hand continuing. "We have an Inland Empire Arbitron market rating of 8.5% and will sell itself since everybody listens to us. We're number one in the Inland Empire and the Stage Coach cowboys are number two." He paused, and then closed, "The job's yours if you want it."

Mitch sighed in relief. "You got a deal. When do I start?"

"Next Monday. The first week you need to spend here with me to learn the business. By the way, where did you learn so much about selling?"

Mitch's face turned dark, his eyes narrowed. "Mostly from my ex-wife. She's a hairdresser and told me all the stories from her customers. She works in the high-class salon."

"What went wrong with your relationship?"

"She started going out with the customers."

Raymond offered his hand to Mitch, and then gave him payroll forms to complete. "Bring these back with you. By the way, the lady who sent you here is my new secretary. She belongs to me. No hanky panky or it'll be your last day." Rays voice froze. "Understand?"

"Okay, Boss. You got a deal." Mitch left. *Damn*, he thought, *I was hoping to make it with Alice.* Then he worried that the job would work out. Little could he imagine he would spend most of his life with Ray, Alice, and the station.

4

Oscar

Mitch answered the door to find Garcia, the animal control officer, with a young assistant. The house was clean, the animal farm gone. A 'for rent' sign was stuck on the freshly mowed and watered lawn.

Mitch greeted Garcia, "Hi Buddy, I see you brought some help. Does the place look neater?" Tammy Wynette's *Stand By Your Man* filled the room. Mitch went over to a radio built into a television console to turn down the volume.

Garcia laughed, "Sure does. It's hard to recognize the old zoo site." He coughed uncomfortably. "Where's your poor snake, Oscar…. Was that his name? Like I said on the phone, the thing is too big to be a Rosie boa, maybe a Burmese python so we'll need to take it away. It's really dangerous to keep. You know…could eat children, pets, that kind of thing."

Mitch walked to the bedroom snake den, officers following. "What'll you guys do with him? I hope you don't put him to sleep. He's been a good little snake. Never hurt a soul. Just grew a little too much since I got him."

"We'll find a home for him," Garcia said. "Maybe a zoo."

Mitch opened the door part way to see that Oscar was located under the bed, his tail sticking out more than a yard. "Can I feed him first? He'll be happy and sleepy afterward. Easier to handle. Besides, since he's going away, it's a 'Last Supper' for him. Please, it's his last meal with me."

The young assistant stared in dread at the creature. Garcia asked, "Jim, what do you think? You're the other end of this thing." Jim nodded.

"One second, guys." Mitch left, returning with a hen chicken in a cage. Oscar stirred from under the bed, slithering to the doorway, his head up tasting the air with his forked tongue. "Watch out, guys. Hungry snake moving!"

They backed out of the way as the snake rapidly followed Mitch to the bathroom. Mitch opened the door, releasing the chicken. The snake swiftly followed; Mitch closing the door behind Oscar's tail. The chicken squawked fiercely. The animal control officers listened, their mouths agape. Suddenly…a deafening silence. "Well, guys," Mitch said, "like a beer or coke while Oscar swallows his meal? You don't want to disturb him now, do you?"

"Don't have much choice, do we?" Garcia headed for the kitchen with his assistant trailing.

Mitch took a tall six-pack of beer out of the small refrigerator then settled around the kitchen table. "I killed a rattlesnake yesterday in the yard. A big one."

"What'd you do with it?" Garcia asked. "Those things are dangerous, even when dead, because of the poison."

"I smashed it with a shovel and cut the head off." He laughed, "I saved it for you." Mitch walked to the sink, lifted out a plastic bag and handed it to Garcia who gingerly stared inside and handed it to Jim who obediently took it at arms length outside to the truck.

"What about the body?" Garcia asks.

"Skinned it. I'll have snake steaks for a week. Want some?" Mitch headed for the refrigerator, beer in hand, stopped, and pointed through the window to a broad gray diamondback skin draped over the porch railing. Garcia shook his head.

"It really tastes good, like chicken, but tougher," said Mitch.

Jim returned. Garcia leaned forward to face Mitch. "I've got a snake story for you." He had Mitch's attention. "I was working for the Forestry Department in Inyo County one time. It was in March or April and the snow was melting. We got a call from the Sheriff about an accident and a rescue mission. It was late and they told us to report wearing heavy boots."

Jim stood up, his face reddened. "I heard this before. Do you have another bathroom?"

"Across from the snake's dining room," Mitch told him, laughing.

Garcia joined in. "This story makes Jim nervous, working with the stuff we do." He drained his beer can, continued. "We'd assembled at the station when the Sheriff arrived and picked up heavy leather gloves and fire throwers."

"Fire throwers?" Mitch asked.

"That's the flamethrower we use to start backfires and burn brush with. Then we drove to a dirt road off the highway, which shut down."

"What happened?"

"A truck accident. Rattlesnakes were everywhere and we had to get the driver out for the Sheriff."

"Rattlesnakes?"

Garcia leans forward in Mitch's face. "Thousands of the motherfuckers! The poor bastard driving the dump truck picked up a load of rocks and dirt from a grading site when it was getting dark…the last load. Well—Garcia paused to take a drink—"the dozer engineer scooped a big load into the truck and left in his pickup. The dump trucker followed him down the road. A few minutes later, the engineer saw the headlights disappear and heard the truck crash." Garcia started another beer.

"What happened?" asked Mitch.

"The poor bastard had his window open and didn't know that his buddy with the cat scooped a whole rattlesnake den into the back of the truck. They didn't see it because it was dark. The snakes crawled into the window while he was driving."

"Jesus. What a way to go!" Mitch exclaimed as he finished his second beer.

"Yeah, we were all night frying snakes to get the poor swollen bastard out of the cab and into the coroner's van. What a scary night watching everybody's back, headlights everywhere, flaming those suckers! Like a horror flick."

Mitch was grinning, produced another six-pack as Jim reappeared.

"Good Playboy magazines in the bathroom," he said, explaining his absence. The subject changed to cat stories. "Do you know," Jim said, "people always panic and call us every time they see a cat in a tree, as if they would starve to death. The trees would be full of cat skeletons if they couldn't get down on their own!"

Mitch got up after looking at the clock and said, "Finish your beer, guys, I need to get to my new job."

"Animal trainer and handler?" Garcia quipped.

Mitch grinned. "No way. I'm gonna be a salesman and disc jock at the COLA Rock and Roll station."

They followed him to the bathroom where he opened the door carefully not to bump the snake lying curled up on the floor. A large lump several feet from his head disturbed the sleek form. Chicken feathers decorated the shower curtain, sink, toilet, and floor. Oscar looked lazily at them as they gingerly picked him up; Mitch behind the head, Jim holding the door open, Garcia near the tail.

"Damn," Garcia exclaimed, "this thing's heavy. The frigging chicken made it even heavier. It's a snake chicken McNugget." He laughed, almost dropping his end.

They staggered out the door to the large cage in the truck. Mitch wiped tears and feathers from his face as they drove off.

Maybe I'll get a dog the next time, he thought, *never a cat*. He envisioned a huge male German shepherd as he dressed for the new job. *I'll name it Oscar.*

5

Mitch Learns The Business

Alice worked at the front desk typing invoices while a programmer recorded music from discs to tape in the back room. Mitch was on the telephone in another room. He hangs up and wanders out to the main room to socialize with Alice. The Beatles are playing *Come Together*. It's almost noon.

"Going stir crazy?" said Alice, seeing the bored look on his face.

"If I don't get some sales soon, the boss will fire me. There has to be a better way to do this than cold calling."

"You've been here almost a month; Ray is getting antsy. If you're smart you'll take the phone book with you and start visiting businesses, appointment or no." Alice continued typing as she talked.

"How does he do it? How can he work all the time?" Mitch looked over at Raymond's corner room. "Does he sleep here, too? That guy is superhuman."

"Nobody works as hard as Ray. Did you know when he was a kid he decided to be in this business and took radio courses in college? This is his life and he's good at it. You hit that one on the head! He used to live with the business before he got the little studio upstairs. Once he actually had a little radio station he operated from a van. Lived there, too. He saved money to buy this station with a partner, Jack Clafner." She stopped and smiled as she continued, "And then he lived with the business in a motel trading radio time for rent, long enough to buy him out."

Mitch stood watching Ray's door as if he would suddenly pop out and tell him to get back to the telephone. "Talk about dedication." Smiling coyly, he asked, "I see you going to lunch with him all the time. Is something going on between you two?"

Alice blushed. "Well, sort of," she said. "He brought me a beautiful tiger cat yesterday." Her tone changed. "Now we're getting off the subject."

Mitch headed for the front door. "You're right. It's none of my business. I'm tired of Rock and Roll music. I'm going to Naugles for lunch. Can't afford to eat downstairs."

In the parking lot, Mitch started the pickup, turned the radio away to the Stage Coach station. Johnny Cash 'Walked the Line' between the prime time endless commercials. An auto dealer ad came on followed by a local furniture retailer, then a restaurant. Mitch was worried about being unemployed and the rent was due next week. The Country-Western station had all of the commercials, yet rated only second for popularity. *These people have all the business and I can't find a single customer,* he thought. Suddenly a big light wracked his consciousness. He hit the horn on the steering wheel and made a u-turn back to the Inn. He just got religion! He parked in front of the public library; raced through the plastered bell tower arched wall, past the roses by the walkway, past the huge brass cannons named after Spanish generals, through the huge open doors of the foyer, past the receptionist and into the courtyard where Ray and Alice had just returned from the buffet.

Mitch rushed up to Raymond, startling him.

"Hey, Mitch, what's got you so excited? Here, sit down with us for a minute? Had lunch yet?"

Mitch was breathless; the other restaurant patrons stared at him. "No time. I need to go upstairs to get my letter pad! I just had a great idea!" He slowed down to catch his breath. He had their attention. "We have higher ratings than the Stage Coach people, right?"

"Sure, Ray said. We're number one."

"We're number one because we have hardly any commercials cluttering the station and people love Rock and Roll, right?" Ray nodded. Mitch continued, "Well, I'm going to record all Stage Coach's commercials. Then contact them."

"But they're already advertising on the other station," Alice said.

"You don't understand. If they're advertising on Stage Coach, they're missing the customers who like Rock and Roll. That's a bigger audience, especially if their ads are already working."

Ray stood up, placed his hand on Mitch's shoulder. "Fantastic idea, Mitch. They can double their exposure. If one works, so will the other."

"Right, boss. The car dealers can sell pickup trucks to the Country-Western fans and sedans and sports cars to the other Rock and Rollers."

"Should've thought of it, myself but I get too buried in the details of operations. That's why I need a smart guy like you out there. I was thinking of letting you go but now we can move together." He pulled out a chair. "Come, join us for lunch. You can get your pad afterward. I also have a portable radio you can listen to… in your little room."

"Okay, Boss."

"I'm so happy for you Mitch," Alice said, smiling with her eyes. "I knew you would do good. And, Ray likes to be called Ray, not the Boss."

"Okay, Boss, I'll call him Ray from now on." He winked as he moved away. Later that day Alice returned from the studio apartment upstairs. Alice was all smiles as she teased the cat on her shoulder, wearing it like a rich woman with a fox fur. She was taunting it as she entered Ray's dimly lit office. Ray looked up with tired reddened eyes, matching the prior days broadcast schedule with the mandatory 24-hour log of music and events.

"Ray, I need some paperclips. Aren't you excited about Mitch's idea?"

"It's about time. I need to get it going here. How many?"

"A dozen or so. I couldn't find any in my desk." She was smiling at the cat that was purring in return. Alice watched as Ray counted out 12 paperclips. "Jeez, Ray. Are you sure you can spare them?" she sarcastically quipped.

Ray stared at her. "We have to watch our expenses. We survive by cutting costs."

Alice noticed the report Ray was compiling. "What's that?"

"A report for the FCC. I also have to do the MOC, ASCAP and BMI for royalties on the music played. Tons of paperwork for the business." He grinned. "Of course, if I don't report all the music played, I don't pay for it, either."

"That's cheating. Don't they ever check up on you?"

"Nope. You see, most stations have tons of clutter with disc jockeys, commercials, and local chatter. I make allowances for the time not wasted, nobody knows the difference." In a lower voice said, "Now, I've told you too much. My father used to put his hand over my mouth and tell me not to talk. Be a listener, he would say. Never tell what you know."

Alice grinned. "That doesn't apply to lovers."

She left for her front desk with the cat and paperclips. Suddenly, an athletically built blonde, wearing a white pleated tennis skirt and Rubidoux Highlanders sweatshirt, burst through the front door. "That's my cat!" she screamed at Alice. "I knew you had him!" She snatched the cat away from Alice. Alice resisted, hanging on to the hindquarters of the startled animal.

"Wait a minute lady!" Alice screamed. "My boss gave me this cat! Ray! Come out here!"

Ray rushed out of his office, confronting the irate woman. "Let go of the cat. It's hers!"

"No way, mister," the athletic blond retorted, standing her ground. "I raised him and you took him from me. Just because you live and work here doesn't give you license to be a catnapper!"

"Cats are free agents," Ray said, matter-of-factly. "The thing was hungry and I fed it. He can pick and choose his master."

"We'll see," the athletic woman announced. "Put him down and let's see who he wants."

Several station employees gathered around for the event. Alice looked around, and then let her end go. The blonde lovingly placed the cat on the floor as she became the coach on the athletic field. "Stand back now!" Everybody backed off as the cat ran directly to the athletic woman who had been carrying a snack around since the cat disappeared. She picked up the cat and stormed out the door. "You catnapping bastards!"

Furious, Alice turned to Ray. "Damn you, Ray! You said you got it from the kids at the supermarket. I have to live with the people here!"

Ray walked away unconcerned. Coldly, he told the onlookers, "Well, as I said, cats are free agents." He returned to his cave where his papers were stored.

The mailman arrived dropping the mail off on Alice's desk. Alice sorted through it and pocketed a thick envelope addressed to her. Then she brought the other mail to Ray. Alice picked up her purse, heading for the washroom down the hall. She opened the envelope and studied the TRW investigative report on Raymond McDade. She smiled to herself. *Just as I thought, the guy's very rich.* His constant demands on her sexuality, her growing fascination about him and the incomprehensible complexities of the business attracted her to him in a possessive way. *He will never leave me for another woman,* she thought.

Raymond sorted through the checks on his desk, smiling at his good fortune. *More money for the new building,* he thought, as he added it to the running total he kept in his head. He looked out at Alice returning from the washroom. Square shouldered with Roman genes and simple demands, Alice commanded the front office. She smiled as she promptly answered a ringing phone. *"She looks good in jeans and works hard. I own her, too,"* muttered Raymond to himself.

6

The Party

Mitch crashed into Ray's office, so excited he could hardly speak. Ray looked up, nonplussed. "I've got a big order." Mitch tossed a purchase order on Ray's desk. Mitch's eyes were shining as Ray read the document.

In a rare emotional moment, Ray congratulated him saying, "Well, son, your first car dealer! I love dealerships. Congratulations! Now get the rest of them! See Alice about the billing particulars."

Mitch headed over to Alice's desk, gave her the purchase order, and took a folded check from his pocket. "Here's a deposit and a big order. It was easier than I thought."

"Going to celebrate tonight?"

"Have to visit the bitch ex tonight at her place. She won't let me visit her at work. She's fighting over alimony or a settlement. She hides all her cash income and tips and then tries to get support money from me."

"How can she get alimony or even a settlement when you don't make anything?

"She knows I can't afford a good lawyer and is hoping I'll agree to pay her something just to get it over with. Just f…harassment." Alice was trying to be supportive because she liked Mitch. "Well, divorces are always tough, honey. When people die everyone remembers the good things. When a person divorces, they remember only the bad."

"I wish she were dead. Then I could remember something good about her. If I could find anything, that is." He remembered the sexual frenzy of the honeymoon year, followed by incessant fighting over money, lifestyle, and finally the evenings when she would come home sexually exhausted. Later it evolved to economics between cuckold Mitch and her nasty lawyers. *Please Lord, let it go away soon,* he wished.

"Mitch, take it easy. Let her go. Let her die in your mind so she can go away."

"I wish she would go away." He left for the day, depressed over confronting the bitch again.

31

He drove to Frank's Place, a beer bar and strip joint in Rubidoux. An hour later, after nursing his fourth beer while watching the stripper, he was still in an ugly mood. A thin girl went through her gyrations, vacantly smiling at the men in the smoke-filled bar. Her eyes avoided them, though, as if she were elsewhere, mesmerized by the pounding noise.

A drunk yelled out to the dancer. "C'mon Suzie, give us some action! Is that all you can do?"

Suzie looked down at him, emerging from her fog. "Got a bunch of quarters?" The drunk handed her a few. "I need more. Everybody, give me your quarters." She stepped off the platform, walking around the tables collecting quarters. One patron reached out for her butt with one hand while offering quarters with the other. "Don't touch," she said smiling while backing off. "You know the rules." She took a Texas longhorn tall-necked beer bottle off a table, and set it near the edge of the stage. The men gathered around her as she stacked the quarters on top of the empty bottle. "Okay guys, don't forget the tip afterwards." She slowly squatted over the stack of quarters, settling down on them. The bottle fell over and the audience booed and yelled at her. Once more she squatted over the quarters. The drunken audience grew louder, crying out encouragement, including Mitch who was now on his fifth beer.

A stocky short-haired man emerged from the crowd, flashing a Sheriff badge. "Hold it there, lady. The show is over. Put some clothes on. I'm arresting you for violation of morality code and indecent exposure in a public place."

The men move back; somebody booed. The bartender elbowed his way through the surprised crowd...shouting at the plain clothes policeman, "What's wrong? We have city approval for our show."

"Not this one," the officer responded. "You violated the pink rule. "You can't show pink flesh in the act. Now clean up and get your customers out. You're out of business. Lock up and come with me, now!" Then the officer called in a unit to collect suspects.

Mitch guzzled his beer, left in a worse mood than when he arrived. He drove to the address on the newer side of town where his wife lived. Loud music and voices issued through the walls and front door of her apartment. Grocery bags overflowed with empty wine bottles and beer cans were stacked to one side, byproducts of a mature party in progress. Mitch knocked loudly; a young braless girl, sporting frosted-teased hair opened the door. Mitch stared at her dark nipples protruding through the thin cotton Lovely Lady Salon T-shirt. "I need to see Judy," Mitch shouted above the noise.

The hairdresser drank from a wine bottle wetting the top of her T-shirt asked, "Who're you, cowboy?"

"I used to be her husband."

The hairdresser snickered and turned away as a male hairdresser, sporting the same T-shirt and a gold earring, arrived. "Whad'ya want?" He demanded.

Mitch could barely hold back his anger. *Who is this clown?* he thought. He wanted to push his way past the clown and confront his ex. He was mellow from five beers on an empty stomach. Mitch spotted his ex inside clinging to a guy wearing the same salon T-shirt. Mitch gritted his teeth, "I need to talk to Judy about a private matter."

The clown smiled with his eyes and mouth, enjoying the drama of the abandoned husband confronting the wayward woman. "You the ex?" clown asked, still blocking the doorway.

"Yeah!"

"Tough shit, asshole! Judy's not seeing anybody tonight, except me. Get lost or I'll call the cops!" Then he slammed the door on Mitch, who stuck his boot in the way.

"Well, fuck you too, buddy!" Mitch said, forcing the door open with his shoulder, and then punching the hairdresser straight in the face with all his might. The clown fell backward, blood gushing from his nose. Screaming partygoers gathered around the downed man as Mitch fled. A familiar female voice in the background could be heard cursing Mitch by name.

Mitch rushed to his car but the door wouldn't open. His hand, throbbing with pain, didn't respond to the door handle. He saw a bone protruding. Goddamn, *I broke my hand on his fucking nose.* He drove to the emergency room at Woodland General Hospital.

Several months later, Ray and Alice were driving down the old strip in Las Vegas. It was early evening. The bustling street was crowded with pawnshops, small motels offering X-rated movies, and souvenir shops. Among them were a few storefront and freestanding wedding chapels offering Elvis and other imaginative Hollywood created themes. One wedding chapel stood out with a lighted gold ball swinging over the parking lot. "I like this one, the Golden Ball Wedding Chapel," said the excited Alice.

An hour later they came out, a legally married couple. "Well, Ray, let's celebrate."

"We can celebrate the year we went together but not this legal process complete with taped music and plastic flowers"

Alice scowled. "You're so cynical. I mean a night on the town for our honeymoon. Let's see a show and gamble, like everybody else." She had stars in her eyes tonight, a night away from the business.

Raymond wasn't in the mood. "Alice, I'm tired. I did most of the driving, you know. Let's go back to the MGM Grand and find a restaurant. We'll stay there."

"I want to gamble. Play the machines. Win something."

Ray caved in. "I'll give you $100 because you'll lose it anyway. Let's go so we can get an early start back to the office tomorrow."

"Can't you ever get away from the business?" This is our honeymoon and romantic night. The business is your mistress and I have to share you with her."

"Never. The business never sleeps. By the way, I've found a nice commercial lot in Hillside. We could build the studio on it one day. Let's look at it when we get back."

Alice put her hand over his mouth to quiet him smiled, and said, "I want a house, Ray. A place for our kids to live and play." As they left the chapel, they kissed. Alice was in love, Ray was in business. They were cursed.

7

The Parrot Returns, November, 1977

At nearby Fontana, Kaiser Steel's World War Two management team ignored changed market conditions, which favored mini-mill electric furnaces that recycled scrap metal with minimal pollution and cheaper high quality imports. Outside Palm Desert, Kaiser's iron ore source, Eagle Mountain, had been reduced to a giant desert crater below water level. Kaiser Steel was under the shadow of bankruptcy and litigation from the Air Pollution Control Board as mismanagement foolishly planned to construct yet another polluting open hearth furnace. The initial losses of high paying union jobs, adversely affected the local economy, especially Mitch at COLA Radio.

Ray woke feeling good. Alice was sleeping soundly, even though the clock said 8AM. He went downstairs to the office, made some calls, and then drove to a realtor's office across town. Returning to the Inn, an image flashed in the rear view mirror. It was his mother's face with her Mona Lisa smile.

"Goodbye, son. I love you. Goodbye." What's that all about? he thought. *Why is she saying goodbye? Maybe she's not well. Maybe she's dying. She was under the doctor's care for a drinking problem.* By the time he reached the parking lot, he was convinced that she'd died. Tears ran down his face uncontrollably at the thought of her thinking of him at her last moment on earth. He felt guilty that he had not been with her and Pops, back in Chicago when they reunited and remarried. Uncontrollable childhood memories flooded his mind as he remembered working for minimum wages in a supermarket produce department during high school to finance his radio collection hobby. His parents, being devout Catholics, dragging him to Mass on Sundays. His passion for radio leading to volunteer for a local radio station in Chicago. He married while in high school and after graduation, studied in radio technology and broadcasting at a local university for almost two years. Two babies in a row forced him to quit college for financial reasons. Then the third child, not his, led to divorce and moving back

with his parents. He remembered the hard years of marriage and shopping for baby clothes and household needs at the Salvation Army Store with the bus rides in the cold and snow to downtown and living on stale day-old bread...really week-old, from the Wonder Bread Outlet. This was the price he paid for his passion to be in the radio business. After quitting college he unloaded auto parts at a rail dock and was able to help his parents financially at home. One day he took a vacation to California with Jack Clafner, his buddy and future partner. When the vacation was over they returned to say goodbye to their families to pursue their fortunes in California. He abandoned his family for fame and fortune.

As Ray turned into the parking lot he swore not to ignore his parents any longer. When he entered the office, the phone rang incessantly and he forgot about his mother.

Later Alice went to Ray's room and handed him a bank deposit slip. She was all smiles. "That was a nice big deposit. You and Mitch are a good team. He gets the order and you finish the deal."

He answered, "Yeah, but I'm still too busy. Mitch should get an assistant because he can do most everything now. Does he have a girlfriend?"

"Not that I know. Sometimes he's a bitch to be around...ever since his ex raked him over the coals on the divorce settlement. It's crazy the way people are over money. I'm glad I'm not like that." She looked thoughtfully at him. "You look ten years younger with that new toupee, Ray. I'll have to watch out for other women now," she said, wagging her hips at him on the way out.

When the phone rang, Alice answered it at the reception desk. She put it on hold, walked over to Ray's doorway. He looked up. "Your father's on the line." Alice's voice broke, "Your mother's passed away today."

Ray stared into space for a moment. "I know," he answered stoically, "She said goodbye to me this morning. I'll fly to Chicago tomorrow, maybe bring Pops back."

Alice stares at him. "How could you know?"

Ray shooed her out of the room, closing the door, and then punched the blinking button, sobbing as his father told him what he already knew.

Late that afternoon Mitch worked at his desk with the door open, partially relieving the claustrophobia from being in the closet-sized space. He responded to the buzzer for an incoming call. "Hello?"

A gruff voice was on the line. "Hey, are you the guy who sold me the parrot?

Mitch paused a minute. "Parrot? Oh gosh, that was years ago."

Gruff man answered. "I had a hell of a time finding you again. Listen to the stupid thing! I'm holding the phone up to the fucking cage." The parrot's voice was in the background 'Squawk, ring, ring, the phone's ringing Vito, answer the phone Vito, squawk.' "This fucking bird talks all day long."

"Well, they're like family."

"Let me tell you mister," The gruff man said. "Ever since I been laid off from Kaiser I'm listening to this fucking bird all day long. My wife made me buy the thing and it's driving me nuts. She walks around the house with the thing on her shoulder like a baby. The whole house is covered with sunflower seeds. I need to know how long they live. It's already outlived the dog Please tell me it doesn't have long to go."

Unable to control his voice, Mitch laughed out loud. "Oh hell, it was a young bird when you bought it. The things live seventy-five years. It'll probably outlive you, even."

"Bullshit! I'll kill the thing first. It's driving me nuts."

Mitch felt sorry for him, but sorrier for the bird. "Look, I'll take him back." The phone went dead and Mitch was talking to himself. Mitch raced past Alice at the front desk. "I'm going to rescue a parrot."

Alice, having heard the conversation, smiled. "I'd go with you to get out of here, but Ray is gone and there's nobody to answer the phone. Bring him back with you."

"Yeah, Alice. The bird that never shuts up in a radio station that never sleeps with Rock and Roll music forever. That's funny. We'll all go mad." He left.

Mitch drove to the rural Fontana neighborhood of small old stucco houses on large acre lots populated by more horses and dogs than people; where most of his animal customers lived and were all connected by family or work. Unless the animal had escaped, been eaten, or died, almost everybody had one of Mitch's animals around their house. A city police car was in front of gruff man's house, the lights flashing. Mitch rushed up to the open front door.

Neighbors crowded around. Mitch peered into the house at an officer confronting an overweight man wearing bib overalls. An equally stout middle-aged woman was sitting on a sofa, crying.

A second police officer walked through the kitchen from the backyard, stopped in the living room. He carried a torn and battered birdcage with bird feathers, blood, and gore clinging to it. His face has a disgusted look as he showed the cage remnants to the first officer, a corporal. Then he held it up for the man with the gruff voice. "You even blew the fence down, must have used both barrels." The corporal was taking notes in a small notebook. "You understand, sir, that it's illegal to discharge a firearm in a populated area?" he said, holding the cage at arm's length. He looked over at the 12-gage shotgun in a corner of the kitchen by the back door. The officer continued, "…. and that it's inhumane to kill animals, especially pets."

The steelworker sat down on his sofa, completely dumbfounded. "That wasn't an animal," he said. "It was a fucking talking bird. The thing drove me nuts!"

The police officer continued as the corporal was writing, "That's no excuse to blow it away with a shotgun. We'll have to take you in with us. I'll take this cage for evidence." He looked at the cage. Unable to keep a straight face, he broke out into a grin.

The corporal spoke out, "By the way mister, what kind of bird was it? I need it for the report. There isn't anything left."

The steelworker answered, "A fucking parrot. A talking bird. Talked even more than the wife." His wife in the background sobbed louder than before. The corporal read the man his rights. Outside, Mitch backed away, retreating through the knot of onlookers. He laughed uncontrollably, even though he loved Talker and Squawker, the bird that talked itself to death.

A month later, Raymond's father Joseph McDade joined them at the Mission Inn. Ray turned the studio apartment over to him and rented a bigger place for Ray and Alice. Joe was worn out, depleted by hard work at menial jobs and now dependent on Social Security. He'd never had a job with benefits. First, as a milkman with a horse and wagon for a dairy which went out of business, then working in a carpet mill for minimum wage. Raymond's mother gave birth to Ray out of wedlock, married and divorced another man, then married Joe when Ray was 11. Later Joe legally adopted his own son. Ray's mother scrubbed floors as a cleaning lady. Joe was happy to join Ray and Alice, after his beloved spaniel had died in the snow outside last winter. Ray and Alice welcomed Joe and gave him the moral and financial support the stooped, tired little man deserved. Joe happily welcomed life with his very successful son and beautiful bride. He couldn't figure out why his son was so successful and prayed to Mary for him every night. If he had known where his son was going, he would have stayed in Chicago.

8

The Toughest Sale

M itch pulled into the dirt parking lot behind the old brick restaurant to meet a hot prospective client for lunch. Pitrozellos was spread out with extensive brickwork in expansive old-world craftsmanship by the Italian founder. The restaurant building adjoined a large patio surrounding a fountain. Mitch entered from the patio. He was feeling good about himself, tall with two inch-heeled boots, tight jeans, and his favorite large silver longhorn belt buckle with gold between the horns.

He approached an elegant hostess, "Do you have reservations?" she asked. He nodded.

"How many for lunch?"

"Frank Scarcella is supposed to meet me."

"Follow me." The hostess led him to a tall, handsome man seated alone in the back wearing a blue denim shirt, jeans, and alligator boots. A brass nameplate on the booth read FRANK SCARCELLA. Frank stood up, hand outstretched.

"You must be Mitch. Glad to meet you." His sincerity and self assurance instantly put Mitch at ease.

"My pleasure. This is my first time here. Nice place."

"Have a seat. I'll tell you about the menu. Everything on the menu is Italian. If you want American or Mexican food, then go to the buffet in the next room. I suggest you take Italian because these people are from the old country, Sicily."

"I'm Italian too, Gallo's my name," Mitch responds, happily. The waitress brought bread, which Frank promptly dipped into a dish of olive oil. "I hear you're having trouble selling your Temecula condos," said Mitch.

"I usually build tract houses locally but somehow we got stuck with new subs on this one. They dropped the ball on some things." He paused, "What's on your mind, cowboy?"

Mitch covered his mouth sounding like the Godfather. "I've got a deal you can't refuse!"

"…Or you'll kill me!" They laughed together.

Mitch leaned forward. "Not quite. Let me do a simple commercial on my radio station COLA to introduce your condos to people out of the area. I can cut a tape with one of my people to show a young couple discovering the new area and your places. Best of all, I'm so sure it will work that if there's no response, I'll tear up the billing!"

"You'll trust me for that? I ran billboard ads all over the Inland Empire and got no response."

"Wrong market. You need people on the move. We have the young crowd. I just need a brochure on the project."

"I have one in my Mercedes but I need to see your billing rates first. He leaned over, speaking softly. "Between you and me, I'm paying a fortune for the construction loan and have to move these units. We track all our ad sources on the visitor sign-in sheet and can let you know when we close a sale on your ad."

They shook hands. A waitress took their orders. The owner followed with his offering of several bottles of the most profitable house wine. Frank ordered red Chianti to go with his red snapper; Mitch ordered a beer for his lasagna.

"Here come the girls," said Frank looking down the aisle. "This is why I come here, the main course. They are the best!"

A column of young scantily clad girls sauntered down the aisle, stopping at each booth, chatting with the businessmen. The first stopped at their table wearing not much more than a smile. "Hi guys," she said. "I'm a Fashionaire model and today I'm wearing a Hawaiian bikini." She held the smile as she turned slowly so they could see the suit and her curves. She had their interest and turned again, rolling her shoulders and lifting her left arm to show the outline of her breasts. "It's only $24.95. Do you like it?" Her parting smile was inviting. She began to move away but Frank stopped her.

"Hey, I'm interested! Here give me a call…take my card." She gave him warm eye contact, and then tucked the card into her bra before moving to the next table. By the time their waitress returned with the meal, Frank had handed out five cards. When they left Frank signed the check for $100 that included a $35 tip.

The next morning Alice and Mitch met in his little office to record the condo commercial. "I see you're in a better mood," Mitch said. "I like you better this way."

"New meds for my nerves. By the way, Ray was pissed off at you for putting the deal together for Frank with the no-payment guarantee."

"Aw, hell, I know it'll work. The secretary will let me know if they sell anything. Besides, there's no cost to the station if it doesn't…just air time."

"I'm just letting you know that Ray doesn't like you taking chances like that. He wants to see you after we tape this thing."

"What about?"

"About his approving all future deals in writing."

"Okay, okay, let's get on with business."

Alice gave him a dirty look. "Don't look at me like that. You earned it. It is his business." She picked up the script.

Mitch closed the door to quiet *Suspicious Minds* by Elvis Prestley and turned on the tape recorder. He cleared his throat. "Honey, I love this place!"

Alice responded, "The beautiful little town with no smog and lots of wide open spaces?"

"No, silly. This beautiful condo with the skylights, the hardwood floors, porcelain kitchen tiles, and double glazed energy efficient windows, too!"

"I just love the big bathrooms with decorator lighting, real Spanish ceramic sinks, and custom Kohler faucets."

Mitch suddenly held up his hand, turned the tape recorder to rewind. "Your voice is falling off. We need to retake. Let's redo the last line stronger."

Several retakes later, Nate Perkins, the newscaster, arrived. Nate was dour, and always well dressed in a dark suit and tie. He maintained the professional well dressed countenance of a television newscaster, but was only a small invisible voice over the airwaves. Mitch nodded to him, and then left for Ray's office. Santa Ana winds rattled a window in the studio. "Well, look what the Santana wind blew in. I'll get Ray to play the Winds of Mariah to lead your broadcast for you, Nate," Alice said with a wink.

Nate rubbed tears out of his eyes, "You stand corrected. Those are Santa Ana winds, lady. Jesus, it's windy and dusty out there! Got some news today for a change…a scoop from the Fire department. An elderly lady trapped by tumbleweed. Yes Sir, the winds blew tumbleweed all around her house and she had to call 911 to get out."

"That's news?" Alice said.

"Well now, McDonalds' went to the trouble of centralizing their fast food trash at a store parking lot in Los Angeles. They wanted to separate the plastic and paper for recycling, an environmental issue. The city clerk shut them down for not having a recycling permit. Bureaucracy wins again." He grinned. "What're you and wheeler-dealer Mitch up to?"

"Doing a tape on a condo project."

"The Scarcella condos?"

"How did you know?"

"Everybody knows they're having problems with poor quality. That's why they're not selling."

"How do these guys get started if they don't do a good job?"

"The family had a huge farm, built a liquor store, bowling alley, and hardware store on it. Then they subdivided the cheap land and came out rich in the construction business. Money covers a lot of mistakes."

"At least we don't guarantee anything over the air." Alice chuckled.

Mitch parked his new pickup next to a Mercedes 450 sedan behind the narrow two-storied adobe-block building. He took a large heavy box from the truck and entered the building from the back, walked up to the second floor past a corridor of offices with labeled doors: bookkeeping, sales and construction. He entered the open door marked President and saw Frank Scarcella seated behind a desk. A crude Formica topped conference table abutted the front of the desk at the center. Mitch placed the box on the table, leaned over to shake Frank's hand, and then sat awkwardly in the small corner between the table and the desk.

Frank looked at his watch, "Well partner, we have fifteen minutes until my six o'clock appointment. What's in the box?"

"COLA coffee cups. You should give something away to get 'em in." He took things out of his pocket, handing them to Frank. "Here's the tape and radio time contract."

Frank studied the contract for a full five minutes, ignoring the coffee cups. Then he smiled. "I don't have time to hear the tape now so I'll turn it over to my brother, Gus. You'll hear from him if he wants to change anything. I don't want anybody coming after me if the deal fails. I'll keep my end up and let you know how well it works. After all, it would only take one condo sale to break even with your contract."

"It's a deal, Buddy."

Frank stood. "Well, be off now. I've got other business tonight. Going home to dinner with wife and family?"

"No, I'm divorced. Someday I'll find the right gal."

"Well, good luck. I used to be married but now I just enjoy my freedom."

They shook hands and Mitch left. He walked downstairs where he recognized a Fashionaire model parking her Volkswagen bug. She was wearing a halter, mini-skirt, high heels and a big smile.

"Hi lady. Got a date with Frank?" Mitch held the glass door open for her.

Boldly, she started singing. "…gonna dance the night away!" and bumped Mitch playfully with her hip as she started up the stairs. Mitch watched her leave, then walked to the truck. Curious, he stood outside his truck for a few minutes. Music suddenly issues from upstairs…*A Whole Lot of Love* by the Led Zeppelin filled the empty office building, the walls throbbing with energy. Mitch started the truck, slowly driving between the building and a boundary wall. He stopped. Looking up through the open passenger window, between the Venetian blind slats, he could see the model dancing on the conference table wearing only her high heel shoes. Frank was pouring liquor from a bottle on his desk. After a few minutes, the girl stopped for a drink, then continued dancing. Then the lights cut out. Mitch drove away, music trailing behind. "Goddamn!" he cursed out loud. "Money buys everything!"

Three months later, Ray found Mitch on the Inn restaurant patio, drinking a Corona beer and eating Mexican buffet food.

Ray patted Mitch on the shoulder, "Congratulations, Mitch!"

"Why?" Mitch asked, turning around, surprised. "Did I win the lottery?"

"I just got a thousand dollar check in the mail from your contractor. You fooled me. Maybe you're just lucky."

Mitch grinned, "Hot dog! I already knew it...the secretary called me. Now you can cut me a check too. Sometimes I know what I'm doing, and sometimes I'm just lucky!"

"Too bad we have to deduct all the COLA coffee cups from the first check. Four cases, wasn't it, before the promotion was over?" He handed Mitch a folded check and left.

Mitch opened the check. His smile evaporated when he saw it was for only twenty-five dollars and change.

9

Alice's Hunger, October 1977

The busy years flowed swiftly as Alice's marriage drifted during her seventh year with Ray. At first she became more engrossed in the business. They shared long hours, money and the admiration people have for the glamorous business. Alice had her own checking account with a decent $5,000 balance so she didn't have to ask Ray for money all the time. Then she noticed that people stopped greeting her warmly, probably because she wouldn't return their greeting. She and Ray began fighting over little things, such as who would go by Pops' apartment with food or to see what he needed. There was no excitement or emotions to share with any children. Trips to Mother's were like a confessional at the Catholic Church that was no longer visited.

Only one event did she look forward to. Mary Sloan, her childhood friend who had married Paul, an Air Force enlisted man, stationed at Norton Air Base in San Bernardino. Ray and Alice's social life consisted of Saturday evening bowling with them or having Sunday barbeques in the yard of their little rented house. During the week Alice would chat with Mary when the stress was overwhelming and they would talk about their teenage years or local happenings.

Finally, the doctor prescribed a sedative to take the edge off Alice's nerves. It did little, however, to help marital problems with Ray. He simply could not satisfy her. After the quick every-night encounter he would roll over leaving her hot and unsatisfied. She was at her insatiable peak of maturity. Sometimes she would rush to the bathroom afterward to finish, which set her up for another encounter that would never happen. She would return to bed to find Ray sleeping, and lay awake for hours, her mind filled with dissatisfaction. She felt she was a snail crawling up a wall to nowhere. She was going nuts.

Ray was willing, but his execution was terrible. Alice would notice him eyeing the Mexican cleaning lady in the office. *Good luck,* she'd think, *save yourself the disappointment by avoiding him.* It would lighten Alice's heart to see small children with their parents at the Inn and she was aware that the glue of marriage commitment was the children that Ray wouldn't let her conceive. The seven-year itch was acutely real for Alice. She kept remembering a sociologist's comment in a woman's magazine that since everybody now lived so long, couples should automatically divorce after ten years and start over again elsewhere. *A honeymoon every ten years,* she thought, *would be great until I get too old, then what?* Her marriage appeared to have termed out ahead of schedule when Paul Sloan called one day to invite her to a local motel. She hesitated, and then agreed.

On that fateful day she told Ray that she was visiting her mother in Bloomington. Instead, she met Paul at a downtown motel where they had several glasses of wine in the restaurant. They went upstairs for the tryst, which was better than with Ray, but still too inhibited.

"Maybe you're too much like a brother," she said when they left. She felt dirty, betraying her childhood friend, Mary. The next week she declined his call, and the affair was over as fast as it started. She avoided his looks the next time she visited with Ray, then it was all but forgotten.

Her life floated past like a thirsty woman adrift in a becalmed boat. *"I'm on a trip to nowhere, getting nothing out of life,"* she'd think, before popping a pill to drift away. She would see Mitch on his everyday trip to nowhere at the office, but he didn't fit any plan. Although he was single, she knew that if she got involved, he would lose his job and it would be worse for her. Ray would immediately detect the attraction. It wasn't that Mitch wasn't attractive, he just didn't fit. So, Alice would avoid him socially, letting him coast along in his own boat in the windless thirsty sea. Meanwhile, he was doing well at his job and bought a house in town. Ray also depended on him for sales, allowing Mitch to come and go so long as he checked in daily.

One day Alice was shopping for groceries when a well-dressed man bumped her carriage by accident.

"Sorry, about that, ma'am," he said, then smiled, "Are you from here?" Alice gave him a cold look as she nodded yes. Realizing he had asked a dumb question, he followed, "Sorry, I should explain. I broke my watch and need to fix it. I'm from out of town and don't know where to go." He had an easy smile that disarmed Alice.

"There's a jewelry shop here in the mall. Maybe they fix watches. At any rate, if you leave it off you might have to be around to pick it up."

"Oh, I come by every month. I'm a manufacturer's rep and visit once a month. Name's Jack, from Washington."

I'm Jennifer. Tell you what; it's only a few minutes away in this mall. I'll take you there, so you don't get lost." She was warming to him.

"Great idea. I appreciate it. Meet you outside." He moved to the register where they rang up toothpaste, candy bars, and deodorant, essentials for a traveling man. He walked outside, Alice followed, with a few items.

"Surprise, it's back here." She led him inside the attached mall entrance where they gazed at the displays they passed. They found the jewelry store, and placed the watch on the counter.

"I'll have it ready in a week," the clerk said.

"I'm on the road and won't be back for a month," Jack the salesman noted. "Would it be okay to pick it up then?"

"That's too long."

"Can I pay for it now and have you mail it?"

"No. I only have an estimate for repairs. It might be more. And then there is handling and insurance."

"I have a solution. I'll pick it up and get it to you when you return," Alice said. "That should satisfy everyone. Here," she told the clerk as she gave him her COLA card, "use my name and number."

Jack beamed, "How wonderful. Thanks so much."

They left, stopping at the food court for a soft drink. "Never eat here, just have a soda from a can. The food and water will kill you!" They laughed, and then exchanged business cards, Alice's with her radio name Jennifer, Rogers.

"I'm staying at the Holiday Inn for three more days. It would be nice to have a companion for dinner or a show. You're so sweet; I'd like to see more of you." When he smiled, he was even more handsome. He reached out to shake her hand.

"I'm married." She smiled, liking his offer. "Let me think about it. Can I call you at the hotel?"

"Better than that, I have a pager. It's on the card."

"Good." She looked at her watch, "Oh, I've got to get back to work."

"By the way," holding her eyes in his, speaking softly. "You didn't say happily married woman, did you?"

Alice looked down for a moment, "I don't have to answer that."

They left the mall, waving as they drove away. Alice's mind was spinning. She couldn't concentrate on her work. Something stirred in her body, something pleasant she hadn't felt for a long time. She paged and he called right back.

They met and went directly to his hotel room, skipping dinner. He was very experienced and their lust overwhelmed them over and over again. They were both insatiable. Time was forgotten until Alice saw it was 10 PM.

"Oh God! Ray will kill me." She ran into the bathroom, showered, and dressed.

"What will you tell your husband?" Jack asked when he kissed her in the doorway.

"That I was shopping."

"Won't he notice you're not bringing anything home?"

She laughed. She dashed out the door, tired but satisfied. When Ray approached her that night, she grimaced, finding his advances almost unendurable.

Their third encounter in early December was even more intense. The lovers talked about missing each other and the long wait between visits. Alice was much more clinging and emotional than Jack.

When Alice left the hotel after their frantic week together, she cried all the way to her car. She felt terribly alone again knowing the marital bond between her and Ray was broken.

10

Alice Escapes, Year-end 1977

Hamburgers sizzled on Paul and Mary Sloan's barbeque this cool afternoon outside their small rented home. The couple was about Alice's age. They relaxed with Ray and Alice in their hot tub. Paul nursed a beer and said, "Well Ray, how's the business? Alice tells Mary you're making big bucks."

Ray flushed at the mention of his business. "We have lots of expenses, too. Just because Alice grew up with your wife doesn't mean she has to tell you all our business." Ray fired a warning look at Alice. "We're buying a house in Hillside and moving the business there. The City took over the Inn and raised the rent. When something breaks they send five guys out to look at it and then take forever to fix it."

"At least the Air Force isn't that slow," Paul replied. "We'd be out of business if we didn't keep our planes flying."

A plume of smoke roiled from the grill as hamburger fat burned. Mary rushed out of the Jacuzzi. Alice followed. Ray watched Paul placing a towel over her shoulders. Alice looked back at him smiling, their eyes connecting. Ray climbed out of the Jacuzzi, his face dark with suspicion. Mary held out a hamburger on a spatula to Ray who took it on a paper plate. Mary and Alice returned to the redwood table where they talked about children.

Paul asked Ray, "you planning to have a family? Is that what the new house is all about?"

"You should know...since you and Mary know all about me." He glared at Paul.

Alice intervened, "Ray, don't get excited now. Nobody knows much about your business, even me." She looked at Paul. "I had surgery to fix a problem, but still Ray doesn't want kids. Besides, he's got me working twenty-four hours a day like him."

Mary said, "Did you know that somebody stole our television and stereo last week? I hate this lousy neighborhood."

"Ray will replace them for you," Alice offered. "We have tons of stuff traded for advertising time. My mother's house is full of electronic stuff we have no place to store." She looked at Ray.

"Sure, you can do me a favor some day in return." Ray's beeper buzzed and he ran inside to call the office. He emerged a minute later. "I can never get away from the business. They call about stupid things, like how to change the program tape even though I showed them a hundred times."

"You're right, Ray," said Alice. "The business never lets you get away."

Suddenly it was Christmas. The office was laced with colored streamers, Christmas cards strung on string from the computer panels and walls, candy was on every desk, Santa Claus and reindeer printed from a computer program were Scotch taped to walls. Christmas songs were playing on the station. But there was no Christmas spirit.

Mitch greeted Alice as he picked up his mail. "Hi, beautiful, Ray here?" then retreated to his corner without waiting for a response. Alice followed, glumly answered. "Ray's looking at some more real estate. Wants more space for the Beaumont station equipment."

"He's always saying that. It would be nice to have more space here, though."

Ray has a Christmas present for you." Alice sat down, comfortable to be in Mitch's company.

"He doesn't believe in Christmas. What's new?"

"Ray's going to make you the station manager and you can hire sales people to work for you."

"Hell, I'd rather be a disc jockey because he'd only hire more minimum wage people."

Alice picked up on his humor. "Sure, Mitch the road killer disc jock. Call in your animal stories." They laughed together, always finding humor in their work.

Mitch looked serious. "By the way, thanks for always bringing me good news before Ray does. I appreciate the insider information. I'll act surprised when he tells me."

"That's because I like you. Best friends and all that."

"I know it's none of my business but maybe you should buy him some clothes. Everybody in the business dresses better."

"Ray won't listen to me. One day he went out and bought that terrible brown suit he wore to our wedding. That was the last suit he wore, Mitch. Sometimes I think you are the only sane person here."

"I went through a crazy period during my divorce when I had all those animals."

"That was just Mitch growing up. Sometimes I wonder what would have happened if I had gone with you instead of Ray. My mother told me to find a guy with money. I guess I tried too hard." Alice's voice was melancholic.

"We'd all be unemployed, that's what!"

"Mitch, sometimes I can't stand Ray. He spends his time counting his money and then works night and day to make more."

"Doesn't he want kids? I think if I had kids my ex and me wouldn't have split."

"Kids don't fit in his world. Not at all. Probably because he couldn't control them. By the way, we have another Christmas party on Saturday. Remember the Christmas party last year?"

"Oh sure, Ray actually spent some money at the Holiday Inn. Dull, though."

"It took him a dozen drinks to warm up, and he still wouldn't let anyone dance with me. I don't want to go to the party Saturday! I have no social life!"

Alice stood up. "I'll be okay. I just get depressed during Christmas. Can you hang around and catch the phone for me? With the holidays there won't be any business this week. I've got some things to take care of. Tell Ray I'll see him later." She walked out without waiting for an answer.

Alice decided not to return. *I can't take it any more,* she thought. *Let Ray have his millions, I need a life.*

Alice took some cosmetics out of her desk, located a prescription, put it in her purse and left. She climbed the stairs and over the walkway to the studio apartment where she made a phone call, then hung up. Five minutes later the phone rang. "I've got to get out of here," she told Jack, the salesman. She packed her stuff and left a note for Ray. An hour later she drew her bank account down to ten dollars, then took the waiting taxi to Ontario airport where she headed for Washington.

After the last two employees left and the evening operator was in place, Ray left the office for the apartment. He wondered where Alice was, since he hadn't seen her after she went to work. Maybe Christmas shopping, he rationalized. "Alice, are you here?" he called. No answer. He went to the tiny kitchen and saw her note on the refrigerator. For a long moment he stared at it, snatching it off the flower magnet that went flying across the room. He read it again in disbelief.

'Ray: I am leaving you. Alice.' "What fucking kind of note is this, lady?" he screamed in anger. He reached for the phone, made a dozen calls. Nobody knew—or was telling—where Alice went, or even knew that she'd left. Ray sat in the chair next to the phone, staring at the opposite wall. Minutes passed before he opened the bedroom closet to find all of her clothes gone. Then he began a murderous rage by screaming at the top of his lungs until the phone rang when the front desk of the Inn called to ask if he had a problem. *I'll kill the son of a bitch she's with,* he thought. *I'll murder him.*

A month later he would fail, this first time, due to inexperience.

11

Jail Time For Ray, January 25, 1978

A month passed with no word from Alice. Ray only left the office to sleep. He'd come and go like a zombie, immersing himself deeper in the business. He was exhausted, depressed, not focused on business affairs…miserable. He dialed 911 which connected to the Woodland Police Department. A female voice answered.

"My wife is missing," Ray said

"How long has she been missing?"

"Almost a month. Twenty-one days now."

"That's a long time. Was there any foul play?"

"No, she left me a note on the refrigerator."

"Well then, we can't do a missing person report if your wife leaves you."

Ray slammed the phone down.

One day there was a short note by mail from her saying that she was living with a girlfriend and working in Washington. She needed some space to think things over.

Ray had mixed emotions. How could she be okay and living with another girl, like a schoolgirl while he was left behind? He didn't believe her. That evening he called her mother and the few people she knew. Alice's mother promptly told Ray to quit calling, that she'd let him know when she knew something. Ray knew she was lying, and hung up abruptly.

His father, Joseph, was bugging him to go back to church on Sundays with him. He asked Ray to drive him to Mass one Sunday morning and convinced him to accompany him each week afterward. Ray found the religion hard to believe but he welcomed the change, not the religious premise.

One afternoon, Lisa, a neighbor, stopped at Ray's office. "I've got to tell you," she said.

Ray looked up with swollen bloodshot eyes. "What?"

She continued slowly, "I held back because Alice is my friend. She and Paul had an affair. Everybody knew but you."

Raymond's face went red. He yelled, "With Paul? How can that be? I talked to Paul and Mary just last week."

Lisa tried to back out of the room to escape his wrath. "Please don't yell at me. I dunno. Only that she told me once that they had a thing going on!" Then she ran out the door.

Ray, knocking papers off his desk with rage, dialed. Paul. Nobody answered. He took out a compact RG .25 caliber automatic from his desk. He made sure it was loaded, and then slid the compact gun into his back pocket. He went back to the apartment to plan his next move.

The next morning, Ray, wearing his brown polyester suit, rang Paul and Mary's doorbell. Paul looked out the door window at him, cautiously opening the door. Mary stood behind Paul. Ray looked at Mary, "I've got a lead on Alice. I need Paul."

"I can't help you now." Paul rubbed his eyes, "It's six in the morning and I need to get to work."

"Come on, it won't take long."

Ray handed over his car keys as Paul followed him outside. Paul got in on the driver's side. Ray entered on the passenger side, pulling the gun on Paul. "Take me to Alice! Where is she? I know you've been having an affair with her for the past four years!"

Paul's mouth opened but no words came out. Ray stuck the gun in Paul's face screaming. "Tell me where she is! I know you're seeing Alice! Where is she?"

Paul's hands were shaking on the steering wheel. He stuttered, "Hold it, Ray! I don't know anything about this. I don't know where she is. Put it away, Ray," he pleaded. Paul felt like an innocent man in a Mafia movie where bystanders get killed for anything.

Ray's voice was now cool but tense. "Tell me where she is or I'll kill you! Where's the apartment you're keeping with her?" Ray's eyes darted back and forth. Spit flew from his mouth.

"You're nuts! There is no apartment. Where did you get that crazy idea?"

"The missing television. You've got a place with her somewhere. I know!" Ray looked away for a moment.

Paul, realizing the futility of the argument, opened the door, ran for his life, shouting to Mary, who had gone back to bed, "Call the police! Call the police, Mary; he's got a gun!"

Paul dashed through the doorway. A shot rang out as a bullet thudded against the closing door. Paul locked it behind him, leaning over hyperventilating. Mary screamed at the 911 operator. Ray pounded and kicked on the door, yelling for Paul to come out. Several long minutes later Ray drove away. Mary was still hysterical on the telephone. Five fearful minutes later, Ray, still enraged, returned again yelling for Paul to come out.

Sirens screamed as three police units arrived. An officer pointed a shotgun at Ray. The others aiming their .45 automatics at him. He was ordered to lay face down on the ground.

Shaking with panic, Ray dropped. He sobbed at the officers standing around him, "I didn't hurt him. You can't blame me. He's sleeping with my wife!" He was almost incoherent. "I just wanted to talk to him. I didn't mean to do it. I've got a gun in my back pocket. Watch out, it's loaded."

An officer stepped forward, took the gun out of Ray's pocket, tossed it aside. He cuffed Ray, then arrested and Mirandized him. Another officer picked up the spent shell in the driveway. Nobody checked the door for the spent slug. They took a report from hysterical Mary and Paul.

Ray was hauled off to the ancient San Bernardino County jail where he was booked and locked up. The arresting officer informed him that he was being held for kidnapping and assault with a deadly weapon. The next morning Ray was formally charged by the judge, posted bail, and left with his attorney Brian Newman.

Several weeks later, Ray left the decrepit courthouse with Brian Newman. Ray wore his polyester brown suit. The white-bearded Brian Newman was dressed in a perfectly fitted navy blue silk Sergio Armani suit, bowtie, and brown and white saddle shoes. "You were lucky, Ray, very lucky."

"But it doesn't solve the problem."

"You mean your missing wife?" He stopped walking to study his client who seemed oblivious to the enormity of the event. "You were lucky your victim was shipped out to Germany on duty. That was pretty serious business."

Ray was unhappy, "They still stuck me with a misdemeanor and probation for firing the gun. Now I have a bad record." They started walking again.

"Better than jail time. You could have lost the business as well as your freedom. A felony conviction could've cost you your FCC license."

Ray smiled. "I see why you never lost a case. They never get past the plea bargain." They approached the acre of parked cars. "Got time for coffee?"

"Sorry, I'm too busy. Besides, I don't want to get my car towed away. I'm in a two hour spot." They shook hands as Brian continued, "My final bill will be in the mail today. Your retainer covered most of it. You should get your $10,000 bail money back by mail within ten days." They separated to find their cars in the sprawling parking lot. Brian turned to Ray for a parting shot. "By the way, they were easy on you because you didn't have a record. Remember that the next time you go crazy again."

Two more fitful months passed. Ray was working in his office on Sunday morning when the phone rang with a collect call from Alice. "Where are you?" asked Ray. "Where are you?"

"I'm in Washington with a friend. I had to get away."

"Was it a man? Answer me, was it a man?" Ray demanded.

"Yes, it was. I can't live alone. Look Ray, I didn't leave you for another man. I left because we didn't have a life there." Alice had left Jack two weeks before and quit her job as a cost clerk in a manufacturing plant. But she dreaded this call to Ray.

Tears flowed from Ray's eyes. "I'll make it up to you. I promise. I'll do whatever it takes."

Alice surrendered. "Like raising a family? Taking time off from this lousy business? Having a normal life, with vacations and holidays like other people?"

"Whatever it takes, honey," he begged. "I even go to church now."

Alice relaxed, "Then come get me in Seattle. I have no money."

Ray was on the next shuttle from Ontario. Six hours later he hardly recognized her with stringy hair and no makeup. She made no attempt to camouflage her fatigue. Her self esteem and pride melted into defeat. She looked down dejectedly after seeing Ray.

I have never seen her like this, he thought, when they met in the airport restaurant. She was wearing a dirty sweat shirt, dirty jeans, tennis shoes wet from the rain, all blanketed by a torn raincoat. He hugged her and they returned to Ontario after midnight.

"Ray, there's something I need to tell you. My mother told me that you tried to kill Paul, when you thought I was with him."

"Oh, forget it. That's over."

"Well, I need to tell you that I was in Washington with another man, not with Paul. He had nothing to do with me. Paul is a nice guy and our friend."

"It wasn't Paul?"

"No."

Ray persisted, "Never anything between you?"

"No," she lied. "Now that we've had our discussion, let's go home. I'm dead tired."

"I need to know."

"Let it go, Ray. I need some peace. Everything is in the past. Let's go home." He grasped her hand, surrendering.

They continued down a passageway to their small fourth floor apartment Alice made tea in the kitchen while Ray went into the small bedroom. He opened a bureau drawer searching out a handful of condoms. He tossed them into a wastebasket near Alice. She smiled at Ray.

"It's about time for children, Ray. I'm lonely. It's been a long trip to nowhere...we need a family."

Ray grasped her shoulders, looked into her eyes. "I love you. Remember that always. I'll do whatever I can to keep you!" Ray now knew she was defeated...and his to plunder and possess.

Alice nodded, broke away, went to the bathroom undressed and showered. A few minutes later she took Ray to the bed where they made love. Afterward she lit a cigarette, a bad habit she had picked up a year ago and hadn't been able to shake off. *At least Ray doesn't complain,* she thought. *He'll do anything for me now.*

Early the next morning, Alice went out to look over their tiny balcony. The cool morning air revitalized her. Memories of the aborted trip to Washington haunted her. She had started a new life there, even setting up a joint bank account with the salesman. But there was a day of reckoning when one of his women showed up and the money was gone.

A brave mocking bird settled on the planter box near her, scratching for breakfast. It was peaceful without Rock and Roll music pounding away in the background. For one of the few times in her life, Alice was at peace with herself. The bird flew away to the fountain below. *Free as a bird,* Alice thought. Suddenly something sour welled up inside her as she realized that she was back where she had started with Ray and the business. She cried, gently at first then sobbed; realizing she was a prisoner in King Ray's castle again. She knew Ray would kill to keep her in his dungeon. By returning, she was his property forever.

12

The Big Business, Spring 1983

Six more years passed before Ray walked through the gated entrance of his new 25,000 square foot two-storied building. A large fountain artfully occupied the grass courtyard which was surrounded by Spanish-tiled structures on two sides.

Ray met with his new accountant, Walter Davis, to give him the grand tour. They walked into the radio station complex that dominated one side of the quadrangle.

The reception area glowed from light radiating through a colored leaded glass skylight high above, spelling out the COLA logo, which was surprisingly similar to the famous soft drink logo. Alice's reception desk was directly inside, behind a glass wall separating banks of built-in radio equipment, where lights flashed, dials glowed, and digital displays with tape reels turned. *Love is a battlefield* by Pat Benatar played over hidden speakers inside, filling the studio and flowing down the hallways. Nate Perkins, in one soundproof studio, was summarizing the live hourly news.

The accountant who always had an honest opinion on everything said, "This is incredible. Nobody else could create a studio this perfect."

Ray smiled. "Follow me, there's more." They walked around the corridor, which surrounded the studio and sound stage island. Ray pointed out the various offices on the outside perimeter. There was an aura of beauty and function in the layout and purpose of the office-studios. Ray proudly explained, "With over 6,000 square feet I was able to build a complete kitchen, bathrooms and showers into the back corner." Ray was truly in his glory, having designed the station for ease of operation and expansion capacity on a great scale. *This is the apex of my life,* he thought. *I have accomplished what few can ever do.* Even Alice was proud of him.

"Gee, a person could live here." Walt said.

"Well, a radio station never sleeps," Ray explained as he opened the door of a corner room housing thousands of 45 and 78 RPM music records and albums. "The music library is my favorite place. It contains the history of Rock and Roll."

Walter pulled a new unopened Beach Boys record off the shelf, replaced it carefully, then the Beatles, then Chuck Berry. "Ray, these records are all new. There must be a dozen of each one! What a collection. They must be worth a fortune!"

Raymond made sure all the edges were all in perfect alignment. "They used to send a dozen new records for each station when they were released. Sometimes they'd even pay us to play them, although that's illegal payola today. I'd copy one on tape and save the others."

"Maybe some day you could give my Kiwanis school kids a tour, as a vocational thing to see what this business is all about."

"Just give me a call first."

They completed the tour and ended up back at Ray's office next to the reception area. Huge piles of paper surrounded the desk. Cabinets had been built into the wall behind to contain the overflow.

Walt, strictly business, cut to the facts. "Ray, tell me about the problem you mentioned on the phone."

"I do my own payroll tax reports." He paused as he handed a sheath of papers to Walt. "I've got tons of mistakes and problems and need you to sort them out for me."

"I'll turn them over to the girls in the office. It doesn't pay to handle this stuff without computers and experience. That's what we're for. I'm glad you decided to turn it over to us."

"I'm not turning the payroll over to you, just the problems. I don't want it out of my control."

"We'll do whatever you want but you realize it would be cheaper to pay us to do the reports then correct it all afterward."

"I guess so but that is the way I do things. I need control over the wages."

Alice opened the door and stuck her smiling face in. "Ray, the electrician is here." Alice was in a good mood because Ray had increased her personal account balance to $10,000."

Ray shooed the accountant away with a future appointment, letting the nervous electrician in, carefully closing the door behind. "I did it. The meter's fixed," said the man.

Ray smiled. "Good. Here's your money."

The electrician counted the hundred dollar bills. "One thousand, good. I don't know you if they find out you switched meters from your house to the business for the cheap utility rates."

"They'll never know. What will be the difference in the rates?"

"About two or three grand a year for this big building." They shook hands.

That evening Ray walked across the office complex parking lot to the tract house he owned next door. He looked back at his row of antique cars parked behind the new office complex-radio station. Smiling, he entered his new home.

Ecclesiastes the Preacher, once said: "that which is crooked cannot be made straight, and to every thing there is a season and a time to get and a time to lose. Raymond would have all his seasons in due time.

13

Cowgirl

Mitch and Nancy met at Aesop's restaurant after work. "You'll love this place," said Mitch. "It used to be a warehouse until some UCR college students made it over."

"It sure is busy."

Mitch asked the receptionist for a booth. She offered a table instead from the large open area behind her. "No, I'll wait," he told her. Turning to Nancy, "I'm sorry about the delay. The booths are worth it," he smiled, "and very private."

"I don't mind," Nancy said. "Now I can unwind from the day at the car dealership. Even though I've got work to do when I get home."

"Work? You have another job?"

"I have a little business making ceramic figures."

"How creative. What kind of ceramics? "

"Cows. I make little ceramic cows." They laughed together.

The waitress summoned them and they followed her through the maze of tables, arriving at an aisle of redwood cubicles. They were made of landscape bender boards cleverly connected together at the top, like Indian teepees.

"Wow, how nice, said Nancy.

They ordered hamburgers and Chablis. "You have an incredible suntan," said Mitch. "I would burn if I spent that much time in the sun."

Nancy whispered, "I'll tell you my secret. I don't spend any time in the sun at all because my little business is inside, like the car dealership."

Mitch was intrigued, "Then how do you do it? How does a lady with beautiful blue eyes and matching blonde hair have such a beautiful tan?" He studied her, noting how her pale blue eyes glowed like lights through contrasting dark skin.

"My other secret," Nancy smiled for him with perfect teeth, another sign of a woman who took great care in her appearance. "I rub olive oil on my skin at least one day a week. It softens and tans at the same time. A perfect remedy for the girl who burns in the sun. In ancient times the Roman women did it." She held her hand out.

Mitch took it. He felt warm all over, not just from the wine. A strange sensation of impatience and anxiety overtook his senses. "You're beautiful, Nancy."

"I think we can be good for each other," she smiled.

Later they left to see Lawrence of Arabia playing nearby in Hillside. Afterward he returned to his lonely house and Nancy left to unload glazed cows and load green ware into her kiln before it cooled.

Friday at noon, the next day, Mitch rushed into the station, waved to Alice who was doing the billing on the Radio Shack computer, picked up his messages on the way to his corner office. Then he picked up his phone, dialed a client. Nancy answered.

"Hi beautiful!" Mitch announced.

"Mitch? You again?"

"I missed you, really."

"But you just left my boss' office an hour ago," she teased.

Mitch's voice betrayed his anxiety. "I still miss you. I've got to tell you that the movie was great last night."

"But you didn't watch the movie. I'll bet you don't even remember the name. You talked the whole time."

"See you tomorrow morning? At your place?"

"Sure, I'll show you my hobby. Got to go, the boss is coming." She hung up.

It was mid-morning when Mitch pulled off the paved country road and parked the truck. White, brown, and black Holstein cows surrounded the fenced building complex. Nancy was standing in front of a round building. When Mitch stepped out of the truck, empty beer cans spilled out, and he stepped into a puddle. He cursed to himself.

Nancy welcomed him with a big smile, somehow knowing he got lost getting there. She led him into the building. "Welcome to the San Jacinto dairy capital of the world. Cow Kingdom, where they outnumber us humans." He nodded, looking around the round building with plastered walls.

"Now you know why I wear boots. I never saw so many cows in my life. Almost ran some of the critters over getting here." Racks of black spotted Holstein ceramic cows lined the floor and walls near several kilns. It was very hot inside.

She handed him a ceramic cow for inspection. "See the spots?" she asked. "Mine have fuzzy black spots on their backs instead of the competition's sharp edges. That's the way it really is, you know. The black fur blends into the brown and white."

Mitch could care less. "Nice cow," he said. "Strange building you have here."

"Sure is. Used to be a milk barn and they hosed it down inside every night. Now they send the milk out someplace in a tanker." She took a bisque cow to the open door, held it up as the sunlight outlined her large bosom hidden behind a loose white blouse. Her broad Nordic frame filled tight lace fringed designer shorts. Supple tanned skin glowed, a full strong face highlighted bright light blue eyes. Her strong physical presence was overpowering.

Mitch reached out hungrily for her, but took the clay cow. He felt a longing that he had forgotten about a long time ago. Sweat burst out on his brow. He was losing control and falling crazily in love. He said jokingly, "Cows everywhere. Does that make you a real cowgirl?"

Nancy responded, looking excitedly at him in tight jeans, longhorn belt buckle, blue denim shirt, hand-tooled boots and belt. "Are you a real cowboy? Say, I just fired up the kiln and the ceramic glaze'll need some time to bake. Let's go inside for a cold drink."

Mitch followed her to a small round house set aside from a larger round house. Cows wandered in a nearby field next to a huge mound of citrus pulp. Strong urine odor permeated the air. "Whew! Tough smell!" He noticed the citrus pulp. "That's what they eat? Swill?"

"Sure. Nothing goes to waste. Besides, the dairy gets it from Sunkist Packers for nothing. It makes the milk a little tart but nobody notices."

They entered the little house, leaving their boots outside. Ceramic cows, other creatures, and bold colorful sunflower plates and mugs were everywhere. A Burmese cat wandered into the living room, meowing for attention. Mitch laughed out loud, put his hand over his mouth to control himself.

"What's so funny? said Nancy. Are you making fun of my place?"

Mitch backed away. "No. No." He could hardly contain himself, "When the cat came in here I was expecting a little cow of sorts. Maybe a cat with fuzzy black spots."

Nancy picked up on the humor. "And little horns? An udder perhaps? You're making fun of poor little Bessie, my mouser."

Mitch sat on the sofa where the cat promptly joined him. Nancy petted the purring cat, and disappeared into the kitchen. She returned with two beers, sat down with the cat between them. Mitch shooed the cat away. Then he kissed Nancy lightly. She put her arm around his neck, drawing him closer. Mitch began unbuttoning her blouse.

"No, don't," she said in false protest.

Mitch ignored her and succeeded despite her token resistance. He kissed her again to quiet her. "I'm looking for a cow tattoo," he said. She laughed but continued the perfunctory struggle.

"You must have spent a long time in parochial school where they teach you to keep away from us, bad boys."

"My mother warned me never to hurry anything," she said, trying vainly to contain his advances. Mitch began unbuttoning her shorts. "No, don't."

Mitch stood up, unbuttoning his jeans. He took it out.

Nancy looked at it, then up at him, smiling. "Oh yes, yes, yes. Fuck me, cowboy!"

14

Business As Usual

After reviewing the corporate tax returns, Walter, the accountant, handed Ray an invoice for $500.

"Let's make a trade, Walt," Ray said. "I have a new $800 Sony video player I got from a client. You'll love it."

"Let me see it," Walt said.

Ray disappeared, returned a minute later with a new-boxed Sony Betamax machine. He opened it for the accountant.

"Looks good," Walt said. "I've never had a movie machine. We have a deal." After shaking hands, Walt stopped at the front desk. "You know, Alice, "your husband has a fine business. Your help with the accounting is a great asset to me and my staff as well."

"Walt, Ray started with nothing. Nobody gave him anything at all. He did it all by himself. His mother scrubbed floors and his father worked in a factory." She had his attention and pushed the print button on the Radio Shack computer for the continuous forms to flow out of the Toshiba printer. "My mother told me to find an older man with money and I did. I left Ray once, but couldn't do it again now that we have the kids and everything. I might have married an ordinary guy like Mitch, but I'm lucky to have Ray."

"He's a brilliant guy and we can all learn by working with him." Walt left with the box under his arm. Alice followed him out to pick up the boys from kindergarten.

Later that day Ray hung up his phone, yelled at Alice. "We've got it! We got the deal!"

Alice rushed into his room, "What deal, Ray? What's got you all excited?"

"Jane DeVera won the Federal Communications Commission licensing award. I have a deal to build the station for her in the desert." Alice stood in the doorway as he continued. "She put in a bid for the Desert Hot Springs A.M. station as a minority, with her husband's money of course, and won the lottery for the license. Now I just have to get her signature for $25,000."

"Another station, Ray? We can't keep up with the ones we have now," Alice said. "Where will you get the time?"

"Not to worry! What a sweet deal for both of us. We'll be broadcasting from Los Angeles, San Bernardino, Woodland, Beaumont, and now the rich Palm Desert. What a network!"

"I didn't think you did well with partnerships after Jack Clafner, your original guy with COLA."

"Well, I'll get her out at the right time. I just need to give her another $40,000 to get the station started after I buy the land."

"What land?"

"I found forty acres in the middle of the desert that would be ideal for a station."

"I don't know how you can handle it all. The last thing you need is another radio station." Alice turned and walked away.

A week later Alice switched Mitch's call from their angry accountant. "Ray screwed me," Walt said.

"Slow down, Walt. What's wrong?"

"He traded my corporate returns for the Sony Beta machine. I didn't know you can't get tapes for them anymore," he paused. "You helped me get his account, what can I do to undo the lousy deal?"

"Sorry about that, buddy. I should have told you about Ray. He is always wheeling and dealing with things. I suggest you let it lie and double the fee next year. Besides, you accepted the deal. Ray will tell you that you should have known better."

Walter abruptly hung up. Mitch stared at the receiver and shook his head.

Alice walked into Ray's room all excited. "Ray, Tropical Travel just agreed to trade some radio time for a trip to Maui, Hawaii! We can have a week's vacation! I can leave the kids with Mother and we can get away! It's our wedding anniversary!"

"Whoa, Alice. Hold your horses. That's nice but I can't get away. Not now."

Alice was pissed off, "I don't believe you," Alice said. "We slave here every day and night, and you won't take a vacation!"

"Maybe you can go with your mother. I can't leave here. Besides I have to look after Pops."

"You can visit your friend Richard Hussack, Alice said. "You can write the trip off as business expense since he manages a station there.

"I'm too busy and don't like flying. Besides, I've got a hot deal Mitch brought in… a sports promoter. He's paying cash for his advertising. There could be a hundred grand in it for me…us. Tax-free money."

"Your doctor said you would have a heart attack if you didn't slow down. When are you going to put us first instead of this business, your mistress?"

Alice went to her desk, picked up a calculating machine, and smashed it against the wall.

Ray stuck his head out of his office. Employees gathered around.

"Fuck you, Ray," she yelled. "Fuck the lousy business! I'm leaving early to pick up the kids at the kindergarten."

Ray watched silently as she stormed out the front door.

On August 31, 1986 Ray and Alice arrived home to see everybody glued to the television set. Alice's mother left, turning the boys over to her.

"Ray, see this," Joseph, his father, called out. "An airplane crashed in Cerritos!" The Aero Mexico DC-9 tragedy was unfolding over the television set. A Piper Cub crashed into the big airliner, causing them both to fall to the ground. Smoke and flames filled the screen. "You've got to see this, Ray. Almost a hundred people are in there!" Ray watched silently, then picked up the Broadcast News magazine, changed his mind, and stared at the television screen hypnotically.

"Oh God, how terrible," Alice said. "All those people dying!" She went into the kitchen, yelled out, "Don't let the kids watch it! John and Josh, go to your rooms. I'll call you for dinner. Go now!"

Ray was still watching television when Alice called him for dinner. "Ray, quit watching the tragedy. The dinner's out."

Ray left the set on, slowly walking away to the dining area. "I'll never fly again after that. It's not safe. My God, Cerritos is only twenty five miles away!"

"People have to fly, Ray. Accidents can happen, just like driving a car."
"A person has no control at all in an airplane. No way out. I won't ever fly again." The phone rang, Ray answered. He smiled when they sat down for dinner. "The realtor says the Hillside house is a done deal. We're moving!"

The family ate pizza. John, the oldest chewed on his piece of pie leaving the crust behind, like a watermelon rind. "John," Alice said, "eat the whole thing. The crust is the best part." John looked back at her without saying a word.

"I can't be like Josh. Nobody can eat like that." John pushed the crust away.

Alice started cutting Josh's pizza into little squares so he could eat them off his plate like any other food. Josh ignored his bigger brother as he resumed fastidious feasting. "Well, John, that's just the way he likes it. At least he eats it all."

Joseph looked at Ray. "Well, at least we'll remember the date of the Aero Mexico crash. The day you bought the new house."

Several months later at the new Hillcrest mansion, Ray watched construction workers completing a five-car garage addition with an upstairs apartment in the back yard. The contractor and helpers were loading a truck from a pile of construction rubble. Ray walked down the drive and handed the contractor an envelope stuffed full of cash. The contractor moved away from his helpers, counting the cash slowly. "This is the biggest job I've ever done for cash. At least I won't need to file a lien for payment."

"Well," Ray said, "I always pay cash. It's cheaper for both of us that way. Besides, we didn't need permits to make a bank happy."

"Or the tax collector." The contractor pocketed the money. "Could make it hard to sell though."

"I'm never leaving here and don't plan to ever sell it. Oh, did you get the job next door where they're grading?"

"Naw. I'm too busy. By the way, if you don't mind my asking, why do you need all five garages back there?"

"For my antique car collection. I belong to the T-Bird Club. Besides there's only four bays after building the bedroom in one and the recreation room up stairs."

The contractor smiled. "That's something I always wanted to do, collect old cars. Do you restore them, too?"

"No. Don't have the time. Just store them away. Sometimes show them. Had them parked at the office, waiting for you to finish."

"Well, you rich guys must have your toys. Bye." The contractor finished up and drove away as Ray walked around his property inspecting the huge swimming pool and tennis court. He completed the yard inspection, walked up the wide driveway to the street where he surveyed the huge five bathroom 5,700 square foot two-storied house. The chocolate trimmed house was architecturally nondescript, the oversized product of a local builder's tract house experience. A mature live Christmas tree carpeted the front lawn with needles minimizing some of the lush landscaping in which lived many birds and a rabbit. Concrete covered most of the back yard, excluding the swimming pool and tennis court, completing Ray's low maintenance requirement.

Ray spotted a large toolbox hidden under a bush on the lot under construction next door. A minute later he lugged it onto the back patio, emptying the tools on the deck.

Alice heard the noise and came outside. "What do you have there, Ray?"

"A toolbox," he answered.

"I can see that, what are you doing with it?"

Ray looked up at her, "I found it next door. Somebody left it."

"Well, return it. Some poor workman left it on the job."

"No. I found it. It's mine."

Alice glared at him, getting angry, "No it's not. The man needs it for his work!"

"Too bad. Finder's keepers."

"Well, I used to wonder about you teaching the boys to steal newspapers from the racks in front of restaurants we go to, but I just found out about the $20 your son John stole from a mailbox down the street."

Ray started to respond but Alice cut him short with her hand pointing angrily.

"He told me you said it was okay to steal it because he found it. You're making him just like you." She paused to take a breath, "You know, Ray, we have a house in the mountains, a million dollar business, fourteen automobiles, our last house rented, this place, and you have to steal a man's tools. You are a greedy selfish man. Sometimes I hate you!"

"But you don't hate my money,"

15

The Tower

Lick It Up by KISS was playing when Ray opened his mail and read a letter from the transmission site property owner. He stormed out of his room to Mitch's office. "Goddamn, Mitch! They raised the rent on the COLA transmission site from $500 to $5,000 a month and I wouldn't pay it." He handed the letter over to Mitch who slowly read it.

"Yeah, your lease ran out. This is really tough news. These guys are really screwing you. Just when everybody is cutting into our market."

"This couldn't happen at a worse time. We lost over twenty-five percent of our market share last year and the advertisers are screaming. Our Arbitron rating was below 4 points last month for the first time I can ever remember." Ray paced in front of Mitch's desk.

"Everybody wants to program Rock and Roll now," Mitch said. There are the oldies rock, soft rock, hard rock, plain rock, classic rock, acid rock, rock-rock, etc. The Stage Coach people are doing well because there isn't enough room for two Country-Western stations. Maybe nothing else works. We should get a disc jockey or do some of those public service announcements that people keep asking for."

"No fucking way! I don't need more overhead. Besides, I can air the public stuff at 3 A.M. when nobody's listening. That satisfies the FCC."

"Sure," Mitch answered. "But not the people who like to know what's going on."

Ray was leaving. "I have other problems. I'm going to the Beaumont station. Want to come?"

"Okay, as long as we get there before the afternoon heat wave. By the way, Ray, I heard something about the electric meter problem. Was there a screw-up by the City?"

Acidly, Ray replied, "I guess there aren't any secrets with Alice around. The electrician switched meters between the house and office when we moved in." He paused, "Well, a month ago City Utilities started checking high usage for residences when they were looking for drug labs. Remember the marijuana farm they found in the desert?"

"Yeah, the papers were full of it. They farmed the pot underground with special lights for sunlight…like the Cheech and Chong movie when they grew the stuff under a swimming pool cover. That was really cool."

Ray gave Mitch an annoyed look. "To make a long story short, they checked the meter and found it was connected to the office…by mistake of course…. At least I got extended terms to pay them back."

Mitch found it hard to keep from smirking. "It seems like most of your deals backfire."

"That's how business is run, Mitch. It's hard. It's always survival."

To Ray's annoyance, Mitch laughed. "Well, Ray, sometimes you would survive better without the survival tactics. Not to change the subject, Ray, but Nancy and I bought a place in Mexico and I'll be taking time off now and then to get away. Business is slow, anyway."

"Damn, Mitch! The business is coming apart and now you want to get away. You're as bad as Alice! I thought you couldn't buy property in Mexico without a Mexican partner?"

"Only beach property needs a partner. We're back from the beach and have good title. Sorry about getting away, boss. Nancy sold the little cow business and we had money to invest. Besides, we love Mexico. By the way, didn't your buddy Tom Hussack buy a station in Hawaii? You should visit him there. Take a vacation."

"Now you do sound like Alice. I'm not leaving my station, not while there are problems here."

They left for the Beaumont site, driving over the freeway for an hour before turning up a long winding dirt road to a small cement block building beside a steel derrick transmission tower. They were in the hills, an area baked by heat, fried in smog, inhabited by coyotes, snakes, rabbits, tumbleweed, poisonous jimson weed, and various cacti. Ray opened the front door unannounced. The air-conditioned interior was filled with electronic equipment and transformers for the tower. A glassed-off room at the opposite end accommodated the elderly local talk show host and control equipment. The host signed off for a minute of commercials as Ray introduced Mitch.

"Hi Ray," the host responded, "Been a long time."

"It takes a lot to get me out here in the boonies." Ray pulled a chair from the corner to face him. Mitch hung behind in the equipment room…

"I thought I'd visit to see if you and your local followers are doing okay. I've got problems with the COLA transmission site lease…need to check it out." Ray coughed nervously, "I may have lost the lease."

"Oh shit, Ray. They can't do that to you. You have a good lease. I saw it."

"Well, they're saying I didn't renew an option. I don't remember seeing it. At least they didn't notify me in time."

"What can you do? Do you have a new site in mind?"

Ray clinched his fists. "I have two months to pay up and move. I refuse to have those bastards blackmail me like this. Maybe you can help me locate another tower site. Call your cowboy friends who own land out there?"

"Sure, boss. I'll ask around and put the word out to my local business listeners. At least this little station is secure. I'd hate to have anything happen here… to me and my chatty audience. Ray, you should negotiate with them. It can't be that bad."

"It is. The notice came from their lawyers. There's no telling who's behind this deal. They want me out. Now with business slowing down, the timing is perfect for them—the bastards."

There was fear in the host's eyes because he knew his little station made no money and the demise of COLA would be the end of it all. He tried to be condescending, and then decided to play it straight. "That's not much notice to move a tower and get up running again. You're screwed, Ray."

Ray stood up. "Nobody screws me and gets away with it! Nobody." He walked swiftly to the car.

Ray and Mitch drove back to the freeway, picked up a lunch-to-go at a Moreno Valley fast food restaurant, then continued for another hour uphill in the San Bernardino foothills. Santa Ana winds whipped up clouds of dust, buffeting the car until they stopped at a ridge area. The side road was lined with steel transmission towers and cement block or tilt-up concrete buildings. They stopped and walked to a chain link fenced area marked COLA, NO TRESPASSING.

Inside the cage was a cement block building and tall tower. "So, this is the other end of the business," Mitch said…

"Yeah, the business end. The mast on the roof of the COLA business center fires a signal to the dish on this tower and boosts it all the way to the big Los Angeles, Orange County, and local markets."

"So, how can you handle losing it?"

Ray looked down at the precious decomposed gravel underfoot. "I'll just have to find someplace else. The problem is that there aren't any other prime sites at this altitude. They're owned by big companies…Wall Street. That's why I think the competition connived to take it away. The bastards!"

"Jesus, Ray, we could be out of business."

"Well, there are always other sites available. The problem is that they aren't always as good, or they need bigger towers 'cause they aren't at a good elevation. I'm going to see if I can hang them up legally until I find a good site." Ray looked away from Mitch. There were tears in his eyes as he thought of the consequences of losing the site. For the first time in his life Ray was facing failure. They walked around the fence again, and then drove away downhill into the cloud of dust, smog, heat, and uncertainty.

Two months later a huge crane lowered the steel COLA tower, the size of an oil derrick but thinner, into the back of a long flatbed truck. The lease had expired. Huge transformers and transmission equipment were being lifted into another truck by a bulldozer. A red flag was attached to the derrick and finally the trucks drove away to the office parking lot. Then the big D-8 Caterpillar tractor ground its way into the small building, collapsing it with a big crash. The Cat ran back and forth until the roof and fence lie besides the cement block rubble. Rebar projected from the rubble at all angles. The 'dozer driver parked with the Cat idling walked over to Ray who was supervising. "Well, boss, anything else?"

"Yeah." Ray pointed to the shattered fence and roof. "Now go back and crush everything until there's nothing left but dust."

"Okay, you're the boss." The operator shook his head as he walked away. He shifted into gear, drove back and forth over the roof, wire fence, and cement blocks until a tangle of rebar, splintered lumber and wire drifted back and forth like a tide over the crushed mass. Raymond gave him a check and drove off, leaving the mess for the new owner.

Ray was on the phone with his engineering firm. The small COLA roof mast was in the hallway. The direct current transformer and other equipment from the transmission site occupied several rooms down the hall. "I'm telling you Ray, the code has changed. We need a new tower and equipment to reinstall the new site. Everything has to be replaced."

"I'll be out of business if we can't get it up and running right away," Ray said. "I'm running on one thousand watts backup now and nobody can hear us anymore. The station's almost dark."

"Well, let me call around to expedite things…but it will be at least two months to get the equipment to the site and you'll still need FCC approval."

"Hurry up then. Be sure to use my engineer, Sam Castleberry to expedite matters. Get that equipment. I can't believe I can't use the old equipment. It's perfectly good. I'll need cost figures for the leasing company."

"There's another problem, too. The Box Canyon site you picked, well, it's a granite hill and it costs a lot to cut into it, drill, and pour heavy cement posts. Too bad you aren't across the street. There's nice alluvial sand and a cement pad could easily be poured and anchored down there."

"I saw the site. That's government property, isn't it?"

"Sure, State Forest property. Too bad you can't talk them into letting you put it there." His voice turned seriously low, "Maybe bribe them."

"Look, I'm desperate. Get the FCC approval for the new equipment. Expedite it, my God! The FCC put us on a special operator's license until I get it back up again. Look, I'll get back to you about going across the street. Bye." He hung up as the intercom buzzed.

"Ray, its West, West, & Klinger. Are you being sued?" Alice asked.

"No, I'm doing the suing for losing the mountain transmission site. I hired the most expensive, biggest law firm in town. I'll take it now." Ray picked up the call, talked for a minute, then hung up. A minute later he took the checkbook off the floor to make out a $10,000 retainer fee.

An hour later Ray called the engineering firm back. "Hey, good news. I made a deal with the State and they'll let me put it across the street."

"That's encouraging. Now to get all the pieces together… Thanks for the help. By the way, what can I do with the old tower? It's in the way on the site."

"Shove it up the ass of the guy who bounced my lease."

Alice led the accountant, Walt, into the office. Ray closed the door behind him as he offered Walt a seat among the piles of papers.
"I think I can help with your cash flow problem," Walt said. "You paid a lot of corporate taxes in the past years. We can get them back."

Ray's interest is piqued, "Really? How come?"

"I can file for a net operating loss section 1044 carry back. We carry current losses back three years and restate the tax returns. This gets you big tax refunds."

"How long will it take?"

"I can use a special form instead of refilling tax returns. Probably only a month because it's a special quick deal."

"Do it. Do it. Let me know how much so I can plan on it."

The accountant noticed a felt-lined brass box on Ray's desk. He picked it up, admiring the Olympic seal and 1984 engraved on the cover. "I'll take $35 off my fees for the nice brass box."

"That was a present for broadcasting the Olympics. Sure, take it. I have no use for it. Just be sure to show the $35 credit on your bill."

"By the way, your bill is huge after this last year's accounting and corporate work. How about paying me in full when you get the refunds?"

"I know, it's been half a year now since I paid you anything. It's okay with me. You know I'm broke 'cause the business is hurting. Besides, your people caught my bookkeeper changing the bank deposits and stealing from us. Christ, all the bad news comes at once."

Mitch popped in and Ray tore into him, "Where the hell have you been these past three days?"

"My back was hurting me so I took a few days off. Nobody's buying any ad time anyhow. We just lost two of our sales guys and one of them was pretty good."

"Well, hang around. I'll have the station up and running soon."

Mitch sat down. He held a small black carved hawk. "Ray, I think our programming sucks. You switched to hard rock and only teenagers like that stuff. I think we should go back to soft rock or oldies."

"No way. Everybody else is using that format." Raymond was focusing on the carving. "We have no choice. Where did you get the bird?"

"From Mexico. The Indians carve them from ironwood and polish them with shoe polish." He handed the heavy carving to Ray who hefted it and gave it back. "Look, Ray, we need to promote the station. Jump start it…have a contest. Maybe offer them some of your T-bird cars for prizes. That'll get some attention."

"Those are my property. I'm not giving them up."

"Well, since things are dead here, I'm taking some time off next month. Call it a vacation."

"Back to Mexico with Nancy?"

"We love hanging there. The people are laid back and friendly. Someday I'll move there." He paused, "By the way, we lost the Ford dealer account. They called and said nobody was listening to the station any more. They want you to turn in the demo, too."

Ray picked up the bird, crashing it down on his desk. "Goddamn it! Can't anything go right?" Mitch picked up his bird and left.

Alice stood in the door as Mitch hurried past her. "I'm going to pick up the kids from school. Don't forget to take the meter readings. I've got to go."

"This is my fucking radio station. I know how to run it."

Alice backed off. She was tired of hearing bad news and working harder as the business soured. "I hate it here. All we do is work all day and night and yell at everybody. I'm going to work somewhere else. I've had it."

Ray watched her leave, leaned his head forward, resting it on his hands until the phone rang minutes later. It was Chief engineer Sam. "Ray, you've got to do something with Domingo Malichera. When I come in nights to work on the equipment he's not there or he's sleeping on the job."

"Hold it now, Sam. Alice hired this guy and there's nothing I can do now. I don't have time to interview and Alice is worn out."

"There's more. Tuesday, he was copying twenty dollar bills on the machine. I asked him what he was doing and he said he was making money. I told him to stop because it was illegal. Do you know what he told me, Ray? He said he couldn't care less and to 'fuck off' and mind my own business."

There was the sound of paper tearing as Ray opened his mail while listening. "Shit. I can't fire him now. Where can I find somebody for minimum wage to baby sit the station for those hours? Who wants to work from midnight on into the morning?"

"Well, I just wanted you to know he's a problem. I think the guy is on drugs or maybe working another job. By the way, we need to find another solution to the Mosely EBS and FMR problem. I suggest we replace the analog units with digital instead of fixing them forever. I heard that some of the vacuum tubes come from Eastern Europe because nobody here makes or uses them anymore."

"Keep fixing them for now. I'm too broke to buy new stuff. Besides, analog is sweet sound compared to digital. I just signed a huge lease for the new Box Springs transmitter. Jesus, all the old COLA equipment was obsolete. I should have paid the exorbitant rent to the bandits and left it alone."

On the way home after work he felt a sharp pain in his chest. He drove on to Woodland Community Hospital and was immediately admitted for a mild heart attack. The end was coming swiftly.

16

Alice In Love, August 1990

At the Beverly Manor Convalescent Home, Alice studied the instructor rather than the dull materials. Tom Winters was reading a handout on elder care for his Licensed Vocational Nursing students. Tom was certainly more interesting than the material: same age as Alice…forty-one, physically strong, gray strands running through his trimmed full beard, shoulder length hair…still dark, and a consistent casual and disarming manner. Today he had on his usual worn jeans, giving the appearance of a person who didn't have money but was comfortable enough without it. He fascinated Alice because he was the exact opposite of Ray. At the end of the class he donned a worn heavy leather motorcycle jacket even though it was hot and smoggy. Alice watched him leave the parking lot on his noisy Harley. *How could he be so happy with next to nothing,* she thought, *while Ray and I have everything and are so miserable?*

She suffered no regrets about leaving the COLA studio. Her freedom was not worth fighting the losing battle with Ray hour by hour. He'd already had a heart attack and she knew that the business would eventually kill him. *I always wanted to be a nurse, to work with people, and have a life of my own,* she thought. She still visited the business weekly to help with the billing but that was all she could take. The kids were growing up and she would take them to the cool Idyllwild mountain cabin on weekends even if Ray stayed behind with his beloved business.

The boys were also interested in sports, so she or Mother would take them to the Little League baseball games after school and on some weekends. Sometimes they would all go bowling together. It was one thing Ray could find time for. Life was changing. Besides, it was good to be with the other women and girls in the nursing class with its handsome instructor. She could feel herself relaxing more and enjoying life for a change.

On the first Saturday in December 1990, Alice located Tom at a booth in Bob's Big Boy Restaurant on University Avenue. Tom stood up, extending his hand. "Alice, I'm so glad you came."

"I'll do anything for a letter of recommendation." She sat down as Tom handed her an unsealed envelope. She read the enclosed letter. "Gosh, Tom. Am I really that good a student? You hardly know me."

"I could see you have character. I can tell by the way you dress and act that you don't need the courses for a job. Most students are here just to find a job or pay their bills." He paused. "This can be a lousy, demanding business with long hours and mediocre wages." He noticed Alice's glazed look at his sincerity. "I saw something special in you because you want to accomplish something with your life." A waitress suddenly appeared and they both placed a luncheon order.

Alice held her hand out to thank Tom. He held it a moment longer than needed. She felt his strength and their eyes met. She was acting school girlishly-shy. "Do you really like me? I mean as a person, not another poor student. I'm a married woman with two children."

"I would say you are a beautiful unhappy married woman trying to get away from something. I was divorced several years ago. My ex was a nice lady, correction...is a nice lady, but I needed my freedom. I live with a co-worker now and have time for myself."

"I am not happy. My husband is married to his business—that is, he is married to me but the business is his mistress. We have no life together."

Tom smiled, grasped the opportunity. "Time for a change then. Would you like to see my place after lunch? Listen to good music on the stereo? Sip a cool glass of wine and forget it all?"

"I've never been with a free spirit like you before. Sounds like an invitation to heaven."

After lunch including two glasses of wine, they drove in her car to his small apartment. The bachelor's quarters were untidy with a minimum of furniture. Tom opened the refrigerator, took out a bottle of White Zinfandel and a package of cigarettes which he put in his jacket pocket on the sofa. Ashtrays overflowing with cigarettes were everywhere. The sink was full of dishes. Fast food wrappers littered the counter, and clothes were stacked in a corner. Alice wandered around peeking in the bedrooms and closets.

Tom handed her a glass of wine and lit up a cigarette. They stood at the counter that separated the kitchen area from the family room. Besides the television and a stereo, there was only a sofa and a stuffed chair behind them. They passed the cigarette back and forth. "You need a housekeeper. You're worse than my boys," Alice admonished.

"No hope," Tom answered. "My roommate's as bad as me."

"Don't you have beds?" Alice couldn't help but comment on his Spartan lifestyle. "Only need a mattress. Someday I'll buy a bed." Tom wandered over to the stereo, placed a classical music tape in it. Smetana's light Slavic dances filled the tiny apartment. "Is this okay?" he asked.

Alice nodded OK. "If you turn to the COLA radio station I'll have to kill you." "Why?"

"Because that's my husband's business and I hate Rock and Roll, especially hard rock, acid rock, and that new rap music." She held up her empty wine glass that Tom refilled along with his. "Gosh, I feel funny. The room is slowing down. I'm floating away." She lifted the glass, swallowing rapidly.

"The room? It's slowing down?" They both laughed as Tom embraced her. He broke off to lead her to the bedroom where he closed the window shade and lit an aromatic candle. Alice followed to the mattress where passion consumed them in slow motion until they lay exhausted and breathless. Afterward she told him, "You're right. You don't need a bed."

A week later the receptionist was buzzing Ray at his office. A man was on the line. "Mr. McDade? I'm from the California Department of Forestry."

"Yes, what can I do for you?" Ray answered dryly.

The state authority, Crane Ballantine, made his startling statement. "Did you know your people put the radio tower on State property?"

Ray flushed with anger, but put on his best 'astonished-innocent' voice. "Hell, no! You're kidding, aren't you? My engineers took care of that."

Ballantine softened his voice, apologetically. "In any event, Mr. McDade, it's definitely in the wrong place. I'll be sending you an official notice requiring that you remove it within thirty days."

"Hell, I'll call my engineering firm right away. They'll be getting back to you. Say, is there any way we can leave it there and pay rent…or send some money to your favorite charity?" He tried a subtle bribe because he mistakenly believed government employees were underpaid. It was rejected with a moment of silence.

"I can't authorize that. You'll have to move it. Too bad. That tower must be 125 feet tall. I'm surprised you didn't know about it. After all, your equipment building is on the other side of the road.

"The tower is really 150 feet high." Ray corrected, and then conceded reluctantly. "Okay, I'll have them fix their mistake."

Ray hung up, pacing up and down the hallway outside. He tripped and cursed as he tried skirting the old 25-foot roof mast lying there. There were tears in his eyes as he called his engineering firm to give them the bad news.

Two months later, in the evening, the transmission signal went out and the station was dark.

The following morning Sam Castleberry and the outside engineer surveyed the transmission tower. The equipment shed was on the opposite side of the dirt road, next to a large rocky slope. "Oh shit," the engineer exclaimed," look at the damage!"

"No wonder we lost transmission last night." Sam said, "The bastards shot up the Mark 4-foot dish at 67 feet, the Mark 6-foot grid at 82 feet, the Scala antenna at 72 feet, and the tip of the Marti antenna at 62 feet." He paused to grasp the situation, "Jesus, they even got the strobe beacon on top. Ray is going to commit suicide on this one. Especially after the audit."

"What audit?"

"The music royalty audit. The station has to pay royalties on all the music we play. Ray must have fudged the reports. I guess he figured they'd never audit him. Well, guess what!"

The engineer went to his truck, returning with a camera. He began taking pictures, talking as he walked about. "They caught up with him? Maybe like the tower on the wrong side of the road?" He stopped, facing Sam. "Tell me, did he really have a deal with the State... pay them off?"

"Naw, I doubt it. Ray just likes taking chances. Like moving the tower again last month."

"Who would shoot up the equipment? The State? That doesn't seem likely."

"Naw, probably the local MoVal gang bangers using it for target practice. Maybe they got tired of shooting at moving targets." He looked down at the hundreds of expended cartridges on the ground. He kicked some of them into the air. "These guys must be better armed than the Green Berets."

"Well, who gets to tell Ray the bad news--that the poor bastard put his new tower in a shooting gallery?"

Sam took a quarter out of his pocket and flipped it in the air. "Heads or tails? Either way, Ray loses." Unknown to Ray, it was the beginning of the end for the business.

17

Alice Escapes, December 1990

Ray entered the mansion with the children carrying popcorn left over from the movies. He noticed the light blinking on the answering machine. He punched the play button listening to the old-fashioned tape play back the recorded message. John's eight-year-old soprano voice answered, "Hello. Sorry me an' my brother an' mommy and Pops [giggle] aren't home now. Leave your number [giggle] or talk to the stupid machine [giggle]." The machine clicked; there now was a male adult voice, "Alice, are you there? [pause] Can you come to the party next week? Please call and let me know, Tom"

Before Ray could digest the message, the phone rang. The evening COLA operator, Bill Waters was in a panic. "Hi Ray. Sorry to bother you."

"Okay, what's the problem?"

"I've got to tell you, this guy Domingo Malichera, the fruitcake, was an hour late last night and I had to stay to one in the morning to keep the station open. You have to do something about him."

"I know, I just have too many problems now. Thanks for telling me." He paused, wanting to replay the Alice message again, "By the way, have you seen Alice. She didn't come home after school today."

"Let me see…she came in for an hour to do the billing and left. That's about two hours ago."

"Well, if you see her send her home. She has kids to look after." He hung up, and then repeated the message over and over again until John asked who Tom was. "Don't know," he honestly answered.

Later that evening, at midnight, Alice quietly opened the back door to the house, tiptoeing inside. Ray was anxiously waiting for her in the kitchen and surprised her when he stood up. "Where the hell have you been?" he demanded, and what's this message on the machine about a party? Who the hell is Tom?" He stood in her face holding the small tape cartridge which was in a small plastic case, up in the air, then pocketing it, "Are you seeing him?"

Alice stood her ground, coolly answered his tirade. "Tom is a guy I went to school with. They're probably having a class Christmas party. Give me a break, Ray. I was with Martha, my schoolmate."

Ray followed her upstairs, "You had better give me a better excuse than that. Are you seeing this guy?"

Alice stopped at the head of the stairs, facing him. "I'm tired. Leave me alone, Ray." Then she went into the bathroom, locked the door to keep Ray out.

A week later, Christmas cards were hanging from three tiers of string on the glass behind the receptionist's desk at the station. A long computer print-out mural of Santa, sleigh, and reindeer outlined with X's on continuous form paper was taped across the front of the receptionist's desk. Bing Crosby was singing, *White Christmas* over the studio speakers. There were no other decorations. The receptionist put through a call from Alice to Ray. "Ray, I'm going to live with my friend Martha. I'm sorry but I need a life of my own."

Ray was flabbergasted, angry, and really furious. He yelled back, "Alice, you can't do this to me, not with the problems here! What about you're fucking children? Are you moving in with that guy, Tom? Tell me!"

"No," Alice calmly replied. "I'll visit the kids and still help with the billing. I just need a break from living with you and the business. I'll get back." The phone disconnected.

Ray, unable to control his anger, threw the phone on the floor. Bill Waters, who had just reported for work, heard the noise, stuck his head in the door. He was six feet tall and grossly overweight for a young man of twenty-three. His job was watching over the station from 4 P.M. to midnight, before the graveyard shift, when he'd be replaced by Domingo Malichera. They both earned minimum wages for the mindless job of making sure the station didn't go dark on their watch and changing program tapes. "Alice left me!" Ray told him. "She left me with the kids."

"Hell of a way to celebrate Christmas, boss. Is there anything I can do? Where's she gone to?" His bulk filled the doorway of Ray's office.

"She left me for another man! After all I've done for her. She left the kids, too. She's screwing another guy."

Waters tried to please Ray. "Yeah, that's tough. Hey, maybe I can go over and beat the shit out of the sucker. I'll whoop him good for you. Where is he?"

Ray rummaged through a pile of papers on his desk, produced a copy of her letter of recommendation from the hospital with Tom's signature on it. "Now don't do anything foolish and get me in trouble. He gets off work at four or five, so maybe you can find out something about him, like where he lives. Alice mentioned he drove a motorcycle so he should be easy to find and follow."

"Yeah, boss. I'll look him up tomorrow and find out where he lives 'n such." Ray reached behind him, taking a colorful red Budweiser racing cap from a cabinet knob where it had hung for several years. He handed it to Bill who went off with a simple smile.

The next afternoon Bill Waters was waiting in the hospital parking lot, near the Harley Davidson. He was sweating profusely even with the windows open. It was the hottest part of the day. He got out, wiped his face with a handkerchief, walked over to the Harley and copied down the license number on a yellow-lined pad. He strolled around the parking lot, returned to his car as Tom and the students suddenly flowed out through the entrance. The motorcycle left with Bill following until it pulled into a gated apartment parking lot a mile away.

Ray was in the office when Bill arrived back at the station. Smiling, he threw a piece of yellow paper on Ray's desk. "Here, boss!"

Ray looked up, "Well, thanks Bill. That was fast. What does the guy look like?"

"A hippie. The guy looks like a hippie. Poor Alice. She's really lost it."

Ray was reading the information from the yellow pad. "I'd like to get even with him and get Alice back."

"I could loosen bolts on his Harley. Yeah, man, or I could tie him to the bumper and drag him around town!"

"That's dumb, Bill. Any better suggestions?"

"Yeah, hire a hooker from University Avenue or a girl from my boarding house cockroach motel 'n set him up. You know, take pictures of them screwing and get them to Alice. Like in the movies... oh, yeah."

Ray acted unconcerned. "I need to think about it before you run off and do anything."

Bill leaned forward, whispering intently, "I could rub him out for you."

Ray was startled by the suggestion. "You mean kill him?"

"Yeah, I know a guy, named The Colonel, a nut from 'Nam who gets the *Soldier of Fortune magazine*. Claims to be a professional hit man, rents a room in my boarding house. He could make him disappear for you. Just call my number. He has a room down the hall."

Ray was silent for a moment. "Bill, thanks for your help. Let it be for now. Have your Colonel call me." Ray started sorting through the pile of unopened mail on his desk, "I have work to do. I've got a lot on my mind, okay?"

"Alright, you're the boss. I sure wouldn't want that guy screwing my woman for very long."

On December 30, Nate Perkins was home calling his news sources to gather information for his prime time evening newscast. The other line rang with Ray calling from the station. "Hi Nate, I need a favor. I need stuff on Tom Winters...for my attorney, you know."

"Sure, as long as it doesn't get me in trouble. What do you need?"

"Whatever dirt you can dig up. Court records, convictions, traffic violations, background, whatever. I might also hire a private investigator. Do what you can. Here's his motorcycle license number…."

Nate wrote it down on the margin of his computerized notes. "Sure, I'll check my sources. Too bad Alice left. I'll miss her. You know, Ray, I can only get public record information, even though I have contacts with the Police Department."

"Okay. Do what you can. Thanks."

Later that week Ray found a note on his desk from Nate. It said that there were two Winters, neither from Woodland. The rest of the note showed a new procedure effective the first of the New Year allowing DMV checks only with the subject's permission. There was also a reminder that today was now in the New Year. Ray absently dropped the note in a drawer instead of throwing it away.

There was a surprise telephone call from Alice. "Ray, I'm coming in after school on Friday's to help you with the billing. I'm okay and want to visit the kids. Don't make them disappear or anything.

"Alice, I love you. There's no way I want to hurt you or the kids. Let's talk when you come by. I want you to come home… to me, John and Josh. They miss you too. Was I that bad a father or husband?"

"Ray, I had to get away. The business was killing me. I can only take so much."

"What about this guy you're seeing? Do you love him? Let's go to a marriage counselor. I'll do anything to make it work for us. Anything at all… Don't you understand?"

"I do miss you and the kids but I need some time away for a while."

"Alice, I love you. I'll see you Friday then?" The phone went dead.

Ray leafed through the phone book yellow pages to the marriage counselor listings. He ripped the page out, put it carefully atop a pile of papers. Then he called his accountant. "Walt, I need a divorce lawyer. Alice and I are having problems."

The accountant took a deep breath. "Sorry to hear that, Ray, that's a surprise. At any rate, I have a lawyer who is a pretty good guy, Daniel Gilbert. Give him a call and tell him I sent you."

"Thanks. By the way, are the corporate returns ready?"

Walter replied with his usual precision, "Just about. By the way, you had a big loss so we can do the NOL refund again because we didn't eat up all the last three years taxes paid when we filed it last year. Like before, you can pay me when you get the refund."

"Okay, I sure could use some extra cash. Just be easy on the bill."

Later that day Bill Waters punched in and showed up in front of Ray's desk. "Hey boss, what's the latest?"

Ray motioned for Bill to close the door. "Alice is still gone. What happened to your mercenary? He didn't call me."

I dunno. That guy's a basket case. I talked with him, you know… He's always talking about all the people he wasted in 'Nam."

"I'm going to get Alice to a marriage counselor and win her back."

"Good deal boss. I liked Alice. Kinda miss her around here. It's awfully quiet without her."

"I miss her, too. Now go look at the scheduling. Make sure we don't have any blank spots on the computer. Close the door, please." A minute later Ray dialed a number. A female answered. "Hullo?"

Ray tried a deep voice over the phone. "Can I speak to the Colonel, please?"

"Colonel?" pause, "Oh, one minute."

A minute later the Colonel was on the phone, "Yeah. Who's this?"

"Hi. Bill Waters works for me. He said you could do a job for me."

"You're Raymond… somebody?" he asked.

"You got it. I need to do away with a guy who's after my wife."

"Well, I'm not sure. How much you paying?"

I'll pay you $1,800 cash to do it."

"I'll think about it."

"Does that mean you aren't interested?"

"Guess so. Bye."

This guy's no professional, Ray thought. "He's a phony bullshitter. Maybe I should do it, myself." Then he remembered the admonishment from his lawyer after the first failure. He rethought his plan. *It will cost too much to have somebody do it. Maybe this guy Tom can be bought off. Something has to be done soon so I can get Alice back. She belongs to me.*

18

Prelude To Murder, January 1991

Raymond and Alice tried on wedding rings at the jewelry store in the Plaza. The proprietor smiled when he opened the safe to bring out his best stock. Alice held a flawless, white two and one-half carat diamond engagement ring up to the light. She noticed the clerk looking at her and Ray.

"We had marital problems and they suggested a remarriage," she said.

Ray put his arm around her waist. "Nothing but the best for this lady." Ray said.

"This is the best." The proprietor said. "Almost three carats each, one of a kind exquisite matching wedding and engagement ring set. Deep European cut…not shallow like American cut made to look bigger, heavy platinum rings and setting." He looked at Ray, and then wrote down a number. "And I'll give you a fantastic deal, too!"

Ray glanced at the paper then took the jeweler's pen, and wrote in a new figure. "Cash price, no sales tax. Take it or leave it."

The jeweler scratched his chin nervously, and then conceded. "Okay. No checks. I need a credit card deposit now." Ray nodded approval. "I'll size them for both of you tomorrow and credit the card when you pay me in cash." They shook hands on the deal. Alice handed the ring back.

A week later, they were seated in a choice table under the magnificent oversized painting of Teddy Roosevelt and his 'Rough Riders' taking Kettle Hill. "The Hearst newspapers thought San Juan Hill sounded better," Ray said.

Alice leaned forward. "Ray, I'm still undecided. I don't think the counseling is going to work for me."

"I know Honey, just take your time. Life can be good again."

"Thanks for the new wedding rings and you're trying so hard to make up and all.

I don't want you to think I don't appreciate what you're doing." She looked away. "I just don't want to lie to you. Maybe I love both of you." She held the jeweled hand up to the candlelight to watch it sparkle.

"I'll make it up to you, Honey. Just see." He reached across to her with his left hand, which had a new wide eternity wedding band encrusted with a row of large baguette diamonds.

Later that evening, back at the mansion, they made love, just like old times. Ray fell asleep, relieved with the knowledge that it was all coming together again and that everything would be all right.

During the night Alice dressed and slipped out of the house. Ray awakened in the morning to find her missing. Tears were running down his face as he screamed for her. "Alice! Alice! Alice! Come back to me." The children came into the bedroom, scared, rubbing eyes; John, a redhead, almost as tall as his father and mother, little dark haired brother Josh following. "Go back to bed," Ray ordered. He found the wedding set on the dresser, looked for a note but didn't find one. He suddenly realized she had made her decision and wasn't coming back. Then calmness prevailed. *"I'll kill the fucker,* Ray thought. *I'll kill him if it's the last thing I do!"*

A month later at the studio Alice called. "Ray, I just got a letter from your attorney. I want to find my own attorney for the divorce."

"Honey, it's easier if we use the same guy to represent us. That way we don't have to pay two lawyers for the same thing."

"The deal sucks, Ray! He's offering a settlement of $300 a month, a house and a car. Your business is worth millions! Before I didn't care about a settlement but after this lousy deal I'm finding my own lawyer and filing on my own. Tell your lawyer to get lost!" The phone disconnected.

Ray picked up the phone, called the attorney. "Alice just called and told me to get lost with the offer. What do we do?"

"Well, I told you so. Now there will be hell to pay. You need to find another attorney because there will be a conflict of interest now. We really have no options in this matter, with community property and all. I'll send you a letter."

"Shit! Now the game begins!" Ray yelled as he slammed the phone down. He called several business connections for a divorce lawyer reference. He made an appointment, wrote it down, tore off a check from the checkbook and went out.

Later that afternoon he was wandering through the equipment room checking the status of the operations. Domingo Malichera came through the front door. Dom is 21, only four foot eleven inches tall, much overweight, cross dressed between gangwear and K-mart, always appeared not quite shaved, had a dull finish to his eyes, thick oily unkempt black hair, and a poor complexion. He had been adopted by an American relative. He was one of God's unfortunates. "Hi Boss. Do ya have my paycheck?"

"Yes, no wonder you're early."

"Need to cash it at the liquor store. Do some shopping before checking in."

They retired to Ray's room where the check was in the center desk drawer. Ray handed it to him. "I heard that Alice left. The guys were talking."

Ray looks harshly at him. "That's my problem."

"I can take care of him for you, boss," Dom said.

"You serious?"

"Sure, been there, done that before."

Ray didn't know what to make of the offer. *Maybe he is a talking fool,* he thought. *The woods are full of them these days.* "Well, I'm going to try some things first, work it out, okay?"

"Sure, Boss. Just give me the word… and some dough to buy a gun."

"By the way, Bill Waters says you're never on time. I know by the time clock. Try to get here on time so other people don't have to wait. Okay?"

"Done deal, Boss. Just let me know and I'll see how to help you."

That evening Ray became obsessed with the thought of another man making love to Alice. For hours he tossed and turned in bed. *I tried to get her back by being nice,* he thought. *Maybe if get rid of this guy Tom, I can get her back. And keep the business, too. After all, she will expect me to sell the business sooner or later because of the community property laws. Then it will be gone, all gone, even before John can work in the business. He is smart and clever like me, there's even a bit of larceny in him which is good because it shows he's always able to take advantage of an opportunity. It's easy to see that he wants to be like me, not his mother. There's no telling what he can do with the business some day with the start I can give him. Then all the pain, embarrassment, and the poverty of living in the worn-out apartment with bad food and no money to pay rent or utilities, will not have been suffered in vain. When you have had nothing, you have everything to gain by taking from other people who have everything. After all, he had put in his free apprenticeship time for the rich radio station people in Chicago and ever since then he has just been taking his money back. At least, John won't have to go through these steps.* Then his mind drifted back to the problem at hand. *The only way out is to scare the shit out of the guy and buy him out. If not, then I'll have to kill him… or have him killed.*

On Friday, Alice skipped visiting the office to do the billing, but called instead. "Ray, I promised the kids we'd go somewhere with them Saturday. Do you want to go to the movies?"

Ray thought a minute and calmly answered. "No. I have a better idea. Let's go bowling. The boys love bowling. Meet you there at noon tomorrow?"

"Yeah. Bring them there and don't feed them. We can all have lunch."

The Scarcella Bowling Alley was connected to the Scarcella Restaurant on one side and the Scarcella Hardware store on the other. Alice, Ray, and the boys, John, eleven and Josh, seven, met at the bowling alley. Ray went to the counter while Alice, with the boys clinging to her, and talking like magpies, went to the takeout counter of the restaurant where it joined the bowling alley. Minutes later they met back at a table behind their lane. Alice was up and guttered her first ball. The children howled; she improved, and then the kids took turns. The game excited them and they finished their hotdogs, French fries, and soft drinks, going back for more. Ray was doing poorly, but didn't care. Then Alice was up again. The children were in line at the restaurant counter. Ray snatched the keys from her purse, unseen. "Honey, I'm going to the bathroom for a minute," he announced, leaving. She nodded as she noted her score. He went toward the bathroom, passed it on the way to the hardware store outside.

At the hardware store he approached the clerk at the counter. "I need a key, please," he said as he struggled to separate the new key from the split steel ring.

The clerk reached out, "No need to take it off the ring, mister. For fifty cents more I'll stamp the 83 on the key, too." Ray nodded and the clerk went to the machine behind the counter and ground out a blank. Two whacks on the numbers and Ray tore out the door.

Back at the bowling alley, he saw he wasn't missed. Later on he inserted her keys back into her purse.

Later that week Ray stood at the receptionist's counter of the Woodland Manor Convalescent home. "Please page Tom Winters for me. It's important."

"Your name?"

"I'm a friend."

The receptionist dialed, "Tom, there's a guy to see you. Says it's important… a friend." She looked at Ray. "He'll be out in a minute. Please have a seat."

"I'll just wait outside," Ray told her as she turned, to make copies on the copying machine behind her.

A few minutes later, Tom Winters came outside where Ray confronted him. "Do you know who I am?"

Tom stood his ground, "No, but I can guess. Alice's husband?"

Ray moved forward. "You are seeing my wife! My wife of over 15 years! Don't you know she's married? Has children…two little boys?"

"She told me all about it," Tom said. "She knows what she's doing…she doesn't want to be married any more."

"You know Tom. I'm really a nice guy… I'll give you $5,000 cash to walk away and leave her alone. $5,000 is a lot of money for a guy like you. What do you say?"

"No way. I'm not interested in your money. If Alice wants to come back to you she can. I'll talk to her tonight. If she returns it won't be for the money, though."

"Well, think about it buddy. Think real hard. It's an easy way out!"

Tom escaped, hurrying back inside. Raymond stared back at him. The receptionist stood nervously behind her counter. "Who's that guy? He's scary. I was going to call the police."

"He's no friend of mine." Tom answered as he hurried back to his classroom.

Early the next morning Ray found the gate to the apartment parking lot locked. He took a credit card out of his wallet, pushed it past the bolt and the gate opened. John and Josh were with him. They took the elevator to the second floor, unlocked and entered apartment number 83. As they stood inside the living room, Ray quickly closed the door. "Well, kids. This is where your mother lives now."

John, always with an opinion of his own, replied, "Gee, Pops. This place is tiny. The guy must be poor."

The invaders walked about picking things up and checking things out. Ray opened a bedroom door, noticed the missing bed. "My bedroom is bigger than this whole place. Look at this, kids."

Josh peeked in, silent. John followed, "No bed even. Just a mattress. Not cool at all! He must be on welfare," he snickered.

Sensitive Josh broke his silence. "I wanna go home." He looked to his brother and father for a way out.

"Okay, Josh. We'll go. Just wanted you to see how poor your mother is since she left us."

"Gosh, Pops, what's wrong with Mom? Is she sick?" John asked.

"Could be. Maybe she'll come home to us again."

Josh noticed a Valentine's card on the counter. He picked it up, studying the padded red heart on it, poking and feeling the velvet with his fingers. He carefully put the card back because his mother's name was signed on the inside. Tears welled up in his eyes. They hastily left for home where Pops would baby sit them for the rest of the administrative school holiday.

That afternoon Ray picked up a call behind the closed door of his office. It was Dom. "Boss. What'd you decide?"

"I'm still negotiating. If we do it, what do we need?"
"How much will you pay me to waste him?"

A number jumped into Ray's mind. "Five thousand."

"Okay," Dom said, "but I need $500 now to get a gun… that's extra."

"I'll leave a check for you on the receptionist's desk tonight. I'll make it look like a loan…a payroll advance. My accountant doesn't like loose ends."

"Yeah, Guy. I'll look around for a gun. Bye for now."

"Don't call me Guy."

Ray hung up, went outside the building, visited tenants, and then returned to his cave, closing the door again. He dialed the Manor, got Tom on the line.

"What do you want? Tom asked. "Why don't you leave me alone?"

"If you don't return my wife, I'm going to kill you!"

Tom, shocked, stuttered, "I t…told you. She d…doesn't want to come back." He recovered his composure somewhat, "She's not property to be bought and sold like a car."

"If she doesn't come back, I'll kill you! You son of a bitch…Wife stealer!" Ray hung up.

Tom slammed the phone down on his desk in a shop area he shared with a co-worker between classes. He picked up a claw hammer, threw it against the wall, leaving a big dent.

"Man, what's that all about? Alice?" The co-worker said.

Her husband's threatening to kill me if she doesn't go back to him."

"Jesus, man. You'd better get a gun."

I have a shotgun at my father's. I guess I'll have to keep it in the place."

"I love you, buddy and would hate to see you get blown away over a woman. I already moved out of our place because of her. Is she worth it?"

"I love her. I took her to visit my ex and the kids last week. She's part of my life now."

"Well, buddy. That fucker thinks he owns her so you better think about it."

Later that week Alice visited the office to do the billing statements. It was 3:30, after her last class. Ray stopped by the billing minicomputer, which was in the equipment room against the receptionist's glass wall and gave Alice a smug look. Alice looked up from her work, "You know, Ray, I'm not coming back. You need to quit talking to Tom about me. You can't buy me back."

"Well, I want you to know I just listed COLA with the Ad Broadcaster. Just for you."

"For how much?"

"Thirty million dollars."

"Gee, that's a lot of money," she paused. "But it won't bring me back. I love Tom and still want the divorce. Besides, my lawyer told me I get half of everything."

"Are you willing to give everything up for him?"

"You've got to understand, I love him, Ray. I can't help it. You can't buy him or scare him away. I just want to be with him." Alice went back to coding and listing sales orders on the computer. She looked up at Ray still standing over her. "There was a time when I would have let you have everything just to get away. Now, after the lousy deal from your lawyer and the way you threatened Tom, I want my share. Now, please leave me alone and let me finish."

Ray went back to his office, closed the door and dialed Dom. "Yeah?"

Ray held his voice down, faced the wall behind his desk. "Did you get the gun?"

"I found a .38 snub nose on the street. A clean stainless steel Rossi. Need more dough though, $500 more."

"Jesus. That's an expensive gun. Okay, I'll meet you tonight before your shift, say 11... This check's from a savings account so I can't leave it lying around."

"Okay, boss. You got it."

Ray noted the time and Dom on his wall calendar. He wandered about the station, making sure everybody was doing their job. Nate Perkins was in the main sound studio. Ray waved at him through the window. Nate came into the hallway. "Hi Ray, how're things with Alice?"

"Fine, she should be coming back any time now."

"Glad to hear it," Nate headed back to his soundproof chamber.

Late that evening at the station, Dom arrived without checking in. Ray ushered him into his office, out of sight of Bill Waters who had an hour left on his shift. Ray handed Dom the second $500 check. They discussed the details of the apartment layout and the timing…. Ray gave him the key and $1,000 more in cash, all hundreds. "Make sure Alice isn't around. I don't want her hurt or involved."

"Cool man." Dom counted the cash again, "No sweat. I got a buddy, Snake, for an assistant. We'll case the place tomorrow. I'll check back when I get the gun and a plan."

"Okay, now stay here and don't forget to punch in at midnight." Ray left to return to the children, and Alice's mother, now living at the mansion.

The next day Raymond received a call from Dom. "Got the gun," he said.

"Good boy."

"Snake and me cased the place yesterday, but didn't get past the parking lot."

"Who's Snake? Anybody see you?"

"Well, an old dame…but we didn't hang around. Snake is the gang name for my buddy, Jason."

"When are you going to do it?"

"Tomorrow afternoon would be cool, Dude."

"Don't Dude me," Ray said. "I'm your boss. Follow him home and nail him there. Okay?"

"Sure, Boss. I'll make sure nobody sees me."

Late that evening while watching television, Ray received a call from Dom. He missed Tom who apparently took the afternoon off or never showed up at work. They waited outside his apartment for hours afterward and didn't see him. They needed a better plan. "We need to get in his place and catch him there." Dom offered.

Ray was determined to kill him. "I'll rent a Budget car and meet you at the motel parking lot across the street on University at 9 tonight. Do you know the car place?"

"Yeah, boss. It's a done deal. How do we get into the apartment… the gates easy?"

"Park in the garage and wait for him upstairs. Take the television and stereo sets. Make it look like a robbery…remember, keep Alice out of it." Ray hung up and continued paying bills from the stack on his desk. *I'll get her back, one way or another,* he thought as he worked into the evening. *Money talks. Everybody can be bought or sold, even Alice.*

19
Murder, February 19, 1991

At 9:30 A.M. Dom and 'Snake' Jason forced the apartment gate lock, parking the rental car inside the enclosure. They looked around; opened the trunk, took ski masks and duct tape out. Then they took the elevator to the second floor, quickly slipping into apartment unit 83. They both wore baseball caps backwards, gang style. The silver duct tape was placed on the counter. Dom ripped the telephone line from the wall. Snake found a shotgun in the kitchen corner. "Hey man, look what I found!"

"Is it loaded?"

Snake pumped the old shotgun and a shell popped out. "Yeah, a twelve gage." He picked the cartridge up and reloaded the gun.

"Let's not use it. Too loud, man. We don't need it 'cause I got the Rossi with hollow point bullets," he grinned." They'll blow him apart. Let's smoke a joint." He took two crumpled thin joints out of a full small tin box and they began smoking.

They waited; the hours passed slowly as the marijuana emptied from the little box. Suddenly, the intercom buzzer connected to the entrance gate rang a signal of two short bursts. Dom went behind the front door, revolver in hand. Snake waited in the kitchen, crouched behind the counter and then snatched the duct tape off the counter. It was 3:30 in the afternoon. Alice entered with a bag of groceries in hand, walked directly to the counter where she put the bag down. She opened the refrigerator door when Snake suddenly appeared, pointing the shotgun at her. She ignored him, thinking it was a joke Tom was playing on her as she placed a carton of cigarettes inside. "Are you Tom's friend, Jeff?" she asked. Snake shook his head, "No!" Alice suddenly panicked. "Is this for real? Take what you want. Don't hurt me!"

"Get on the floor, and put your fucking head down." Snake said as he put his knee in her back.

Dom came behind her, pushed her head down, taped her eyes with the duct tape, and ran the tape from the top to the bottom of her face over her nose. Then he put more tape across her mouth, poking small holes for her nostrils and put a ski mask over her head. He wrenched her hands behind her back, tying them. He led her to the bedroom mattress, pushed her face down on it, and taped her ankles. Alice immediately experienced trouble breathing through the tape holes, making a noisy struggle. Her heart beat so hard she thought she would die. "Shut up or we'll kill you!" Snake ordered.

Dom turned her over, cut a slit in the duct tape over her mouth. He disguised his voice. "What's your name? Do you live here?" he asked.

"Take what you want and go," she cried.

"Keep your mouth shut, lady or we'll kill you."

Snake backed off, and headed for the door. Dom turned, grabbing his shirt. "Don't chicken out on me now!"

They left the bedroom, closing the door behind them. A minute later Snake returned, and cut Alice's tank top up the back, then one of her bra straps. He went out and returned a few minutes later, rolled her over face up, cut the other bra strap. Snake reached out fondling her when Dom suddenly hit him from behind. Snake looked over his shoulder with a startled look. Dom had another fist ready for him along with a dirty look. Alice cried in terror, afraid of the rape to follow. Dom put his hand over her taped mouth. "Shut up. We're not going to hurt you." They left and closed the door. It was silent again.

The intercom buzzed twice at 4 P.M. breaking the silence. "Turn the TV and shower on, make noise," Snake said. A minute later Tom unlocked the front door. It stuck as he pushed it open. "Oh, shit." Snake whispered.

Tom stepped inside to be confronted by Dom. "Oh God!" he cried as he was pushed to the sofa, the door closed behind him. Dom held the pistol to his head and pulled the trigger, shooting downward. The bullet struck the left temple without exiting. The killers immediately left carrying the TV and stereo. Tom was left struggling on the sofa.

Alice screamed hysterically, "Tom! Tom! Tom!" She rolled off the mattress feet first, managing to stand by doubling over and slowly straightening out. Total panic… now screaming and crying. Taking tiny steps with bound feet she inched the few feet to the bedroom door, turning around to open it and step aside. She inched and hopped across the kitchen. Still blindfolded she located the phone on the counter, knocked it off the counter behind her, but could not hear a dial tone. There were noises outside the apartment, people talking loudly. She inched and hopped across the floor, passing Tom, but not seeing or hearing him above her own screams. Tom was coughing up blood, which was spewing over the wall, curtains, and floor as a hemorrhage filled his lungs, drowning him. Alice reached the front door, opening it with taped hands behind her.

She stumbled outside screaming for help, still crying. A woman screamed on seeing Alice half-naked. Endless long minutes passed, nobody offered to help. Alice continued screaming and sobbing until the police arrived twenty minutes later. A rookie female officer pointed her gun at Alice. "Are you carrying a weapon? Do you have a gun?" she asked.

"No! No! No!" sobbed Alice, "Are you crazy?"

"Hop out of the way! This way! Get out of the doorway!"

Alice hip-hopped toward the voice. The officer patted her down. Other police officers followed and one produced a mirror to look around the doorway before entering. Cautiously he entered, gun still drawn, to find Tom dead in a pool of blood.

The police now ignored Alice. A compassionate neighbor woman tied Alice's tank top back up, took the tape off her face and untied her. Paramedics rushed by. The evidence team arrived. Police were coming and going leaving Alice standing outside on the walkway.

An officer asked her, "What does he look like? What was he wearing?"

Alice lost it. "No," she sobbed. "Let me see him!" She was led to the apartment manager's place instead. As she entered she turned and saw the coroner's team coming up the stairs. She screamed hysterically knowing Tom was dead. The apartment manager's place became a local command center filled with police. A female officer approached Alice at a kitchen table. "Tell me all," she directed. Still hysterical and breathless, Alice recited her story.

A male police officer approached. "Tell me all," he demanded and Alice told it over again.

Detective Nelson, aged forty-five, entered the room. He was wearing a dark business suit. He took pride in being professional and not needing the uniform any more. He was of above average height, solid but not overweight, wore only slip-on penny loafers and no-iron shirts of any color. His friendly, casual demeanor had disarmed many a criminal and made many friends. "Tell me everything, Ma'am. Did you and Tom do drugs? There was marijuana in the apartment."

Alice shook her head no. "I could use a cigarette, though."

"I don't smoke. It would ruin my golf score. Let's see what I can do," he said as he procured a cigarette from the apartment manager. Alice told her story as before. "I know this is an ordeal… you need to come to the station with me so we can finish the interview. Okay?" he asked.

Alice looked at him, liked his soft, but firm, manner, and nodded. "Could you please get me the carton of cigarettes from the refrigerator? I'm going to need them," she said.

An hour later at the police station Nelson turned the tape recorder on, identified himself, Alice, the time, and place. Alice was regaining her composure. He began, "Ma'am, who could do such a thing?"

"Ray, my husband. Tom told me that Ray offered him $5,000 to leave me. He also threatened to kill Tom."

"Jealous husbands are always murdering people," the detective muttered. "Please describe the men in the apartment."

Alice lit another cigarette. Her hand was shaking. "The guy with the shotgun was left handed and had glasses. I could see some freckles, too. He wore a polo shirt and was smaller than I am. The other guy was always behind me and I couldn't see anything, just hear him. I think he was in charge, though.

"Very good Ma'am. It's amazing how many little things you can remember when you clear your mind. Please continue." For another hour the interrogation continued until the ash tray in front of Alice was overflowing. The machine clicked off. "Mrs. McDade. It's been a long terrible day for you. I have what I need for now. Can we take you home or someplace?"

"I'd like to stay with my aunt and uncle tonight in Redlands. I can't go home now."

"I understand. Thanks for your cooperation." They shook hands. She took his card as he turned her over to an anxious explorer scout for delivery to Redlands. Nelson turned to another officer. "Tomorrow is Raymond's day with us."

That evening Ray picked up the ringing phone at the station. It was Dom. "Man, the job is done," he said.

"I don't believe you." Ray said.

"Yeah, it's done. I need the money now 'n you need to get the car back."

Ray recovered his surprise; "I'll meet you at the car in an hour. Have to get the cash first, $3,000."

"Hey," Dom exclaims, "you said $5,000 to waste him."

"Sure, but I already gave you $1,000 for the gun and another $1,000 cash."

"Oh, shit. I forgot."

Ray smiled to himself as he went to the filing cabinet he used for a safe. *I screwed him out of $1,000 for the gun that was really extra,* he thought. *This guy Dom, is really simple.* Raymond didn't know it, but he had bought a gun by and for the COLA Corporation which would complicate his life later on.

At the rental sedan in front of the motel, Ray handed an envelope to Dom who carefully counted the cash. Then Ray drove the car across the street, dropped it off at the rental office. He walked back across the street, drove away in his old Lincoln. He had mixed thoughts, and then his face lit up. *When Alice comes home,* he thought, *I won't have to sell the business. I'll make it up to her and it'll be like before, now that Tom is out of the way. She'll probably be pretty good in bed again, like after she went to Washington.* He smiled all the way home to the children.

The next afternoon at the police station Detective Nelson met Ray in the interrogation room. "Mr. McDade, do you know why you're here?"

"Sure, Alice called me last night."

"Where were you yesterday, all day?"

"I went to work. Was there all day," Ray said.

"Any witnesses?"

"Four employees who were with me all day long. The receptionist, engineer, a sales person, and the newscaster."

What were you doing?"

"I was programming music for the next month. It's very important and nobody can do it but me," Raymond said.

"Did you know the deceased, Tom Winters?"

"The guy my wife was seeing? Is that his name?" Ray played dumb, "No, never met him."

"You know, Mr. McDade, if you're lying we'll find out. A terrible crime was committed and you're a suspect." *Unfortunate we have to be polite to people like this,* the detective thought. *I know this smug bastard did it, I can tell by looking at his eyes. After all, this was no robbery because Alice's money in her purse wasn't touched or jewelry stolen. Somebody also told the bad guys not to touch her; otherwise they would have raped and killed her, too.*

"I'm sorry that this guy, Winters, is it, was killed, but I had nothing to do with it. Maybe he had another woman and a boyfriend did him in," Raymond said.

The interrogation continued for several hours longer. Finally, detective Wilson pulled the plug. "Mr. McDade, we're still gathering evidence. Please don't leave town for a while. We'll get back if we need you."

"Sure, I hope you catch the guy who did this thing."

The detective nodded, "We always do," as his best suspect left.

At the Woodland National Cemetery on the following bright Sunday morning, Tom Winters received a military funeral. After the honor guard fired the farewell salute to the Viet Nam Veteran his ex-wife was given the folded flag. Alice was with the family. Raymond was also there. Alice avoided him by sitting in the front row with the family. When the ceremony was over she confronted Ray. "I told you not to come," she said.

"I told you, I'm innocent." He tried to hold her hand.

"Keep away from me!" she screamed.

"I love you. If you don't come back. I'll commit suicide. I swear.

Alice stared at him in disbelief then ran to her car.

That evening Alice wanted to die. She sat in a stuffed chair at her aunt's alone, crying. The lights went out when her aunt went to bed. A nightlight glowed on a wall. Alice fell asleep. She dreamed that she visited God. He had blondish-brown hair and a beard. His trimmed white robes flowed and blew about His ethereal presence. There was a wondrous white light about and behind Him which filled the air. He stood in mid air, barefoot, holding out long arms to her, long fingers reached for her. Alice felt peaceful and floated in the presence of God. There was no facial movement as He spoke without speaking. He was Supreme, overpowering, but had a calm voice. "I'm here for you. Come to me if you are ready." Alice immediately realized that she was dying and would leave the boys without a mother. She chose to live and suddenly the dream was gone and she woke up. She now felt alive and energized, ready to go on with her life, to do what she had to for survival.

Ray was on the phone in the office. "Yes, I know Mrs. DeVera; I know we had a deal to build the Desert Hot Springs station together.

"What's holding you up?"

"Well, I had some financial problems. There's a recession going on."

"I don't want excuses. Either you immediately build the station or release me from the partnership agreement. Which do you want?"

"Okay. I'll release you from the deal. Send me a check for my interest, the $25,000, and I'll let it go."

"No way, Jose! You release it now or I'll sue you. You're in default for non-performance. I'll have my lawyer send you the papers. Comply or I'll sue you."

"Lady, you talk like a lawyer. Give me a week to see what I can do."

"No deal. I already have another partner. Besides, my husband's a lawyer and he says you lost the deal."

"Okay," Ray said in defeat. "Send the release."

"By the way, I would like to buy the land you bought for the station."

"Get lost, lady."

He hung up, then grabbed a handful of pencils from a cup on his desk, snapped them and tossed them across the room.

The afternoon mail arrived. Ray sorted through it for checks, but instead found a letter from West, West & Klinger. Ray tore into it, reading, 'Dear Mr. McDade, the suit we filed in your behalf for the transmission site lease has been denied a trial. If you have additional information to reopen the case please contact us. Otherwise, consider the case closed. It was signed, 0. Reginald Smith, Senior Partner.' Enclosed was an invoice for $60,000 less the deposit of $10,000 leaving $50,000 still owing. Ray tore through the office screaming at the employees and throwing things about.

Two weeks later, Ray was at home reading the Broadcast News when the phone rang. John left the TV, with Josh following, picked it up in the kitchen. Ray continued reading. John rushed out of the kitchen, "Moms on the phone. She wants to talk to Josh."

Ray threw the paper down, rushed into the kitchen, and snatched the phone from Josh who began crying.

"Alice, are you okay? I'm worried about you. I'll commit suicide if you don't come home. I mean it."

"Ray, I'm going crazy living with my aunt. I miss the kids and Mother so much. I do want to believe that you didn't do it to Tom. The past weeks were hell. I want to come home."

Ray had tears in his eyes, "Oh, thank God! I love you Alice. You know how much I miss you! When... how soon are you coming back?"

"Tonight," she sighed. "I'll be home tonight. But I get the extra bedroom; I want you to keep away from me." The dial tone came on as she disconnected.

Ray rushed into the living room, shut the TV off. "Hey kids, let's have a party! Your mother's coming home. Tell Pops. He's in his room!"

The kids shriek in jubilation. "Come on. Let's go to the supermarket for a cake and ice cream."

"Can we get balloons, too?" Josh asked.

"Sure kid, anything you want."

A week later, while tidying up the master bedroom, Alice discovered an electrical box connected to a tape recorder that was wired to the telephone outlet and hidden under the bed.

Before the month was over, she moved back into the master bedroom with Ray. Her period was two weeks late because of the trauma. At first she believed she was pregnant, hoping and praying it was Tom's. She would wake up screaming with nightmares of the murder. She felt alone and vulnerable, especially with the haunting thought of the murderers out there somewhere, free and loose… to kill her, the witness. Then her period returned, delayed by intense stress and Alice became more depressed.

Ray suddenly became a family man, leaving work earlier with the employees, taking the boys to see the airplanes at the 'Lindy' air museum in San Diego, Disneyland, and trips to the San Diego Zoo. They went to the Ramona Festival in Hemet; the children enjoying the Cowboys and Indians but bored by the dancing and singing. He took them to Saturday little league games and started taking them to the Catholic Church with elderly Joseph for Sunday mass.

A tense unnatural peace prevailed over the household. Alice was now on Prozac, still feeling imprisoned in the mansion with Ray. Ray struggled with the business, haunted by the murder, trying to wish the consequences away while looking over his shoulder for the Police detectives.

Meanwhile the detectives gathered their evidence. Detective Nelson talked to the receptionist at the Manor and with Tom's co-worker who showed him the big dent in the office wall where the hammer hit. Then he interviewed the apartment tenants where he met the lady who observed the murderers casing the place before the crime, and another lady who saw them enter the apartment on the morning of the murder. He spoke to the radio station employees and was amazed to learn about the Colonel's death offer, possible involvement of Bill Waters and Dom. Nelson interviewed the victim's father who had known about the death threat and had advised him to hide his motorcycle and keep the shotgun handy. He interviewed the victim's ex-wife who still had warm feelings for Tom, met his two children, who loved him so much that they were having severe emotional problems coping. Somewhere in the interviewing process Nelson realized that Tom was loved by everybody, except Raymond McDade.

"This guy, Tom was a really nice person; they murdered a good guy," Nelson told his partner Carlson as they compared notes in the squad room. Detective Carlson was a heavy-set man with twenty-five year's experience, the same as Nelson. Carlson was the department intellectual, always reading a book, and had published his own book on police self-defense tactics, a primer on keeping alive while on duty. The two detectives were the cream of the police department. "Sometimes a bad guy gets killed and it seems a shame to put the killer away for doing the world a favor," Nelson concluded.

"Unless it's another bad guy," Carlson added.

"Sure, but this guy McDade, nobody knows him or likes him. He just sits in his little office scheming and counting his money. It's just not fair; him taking his money to try and buy his wife back from this guy."

"... and using the same money to pay a murderer when he won't go away."

Nelson reached out to make a pact with Carlson. "Let's swear to put this guy away, no matter what." The pact was solemnly completed with a handshake.

Detective Carlson visited the coroner, watched him insert a rod into the bullet hole, take a picture, then saw the skull opened to extract the bullet from inside the opposite side. The coroner, talking into a recorder, explained that the cause of death was the victim drowning in his own blood from a severed artery. The detective then carefully took the washed bullet, put it into a paper jewelry box, marked the box and sent it off to the crime lab in Sacramento.

Nelson and Carlson waited for a break in the case. They needed hard evidence to satisfy the discovery requirements of the prosecutor, Deputy District Attorney Lucas Carranza, whose name appeared on all the legal paperwork of the case and who would not go to court without a plea bargain or winning a trial. Lucas, of humble beginnings led a simple life with a highly religious wife who brought him back to earth from the job. Several highly educated generations removed from Latino immigrants, he was of stocky build with full face and lightly tanned native skin. He had the deceiving appearance of an ordinary man with an extraordinary occupation. He was driven by his profession and had a true passion for justice. Lucas had never lost a case and was called 'professor' by his associates because he was relentless and thorough about discovery evidence and procedure. He was the prosecution sniper, the unseen enemy soldier, dreaded because he always got his man. The District Attorney always gave him the high profile cases to close. His detectives respected and admired him even though he was impossible to work for. He drove himself for perfection and expected it from his associates. Lucas waited patiently as the detectives gathered data on the complicated rich man, McDade. The months passed slowly. January through May of 1991 saw no satisfactory hard evidence to arrest. Lucas patiently kept busy with other cases, including a new mass murder case. He was never in a hurry because he had time on his side. He wouldn't need to wait much longer before his work would begin in earnest.

20
Juvenile Execution, May 29, 1991

Dom parked his old Camaro in front of the Moreno Valley house where teenagers Eduardo Sanchez and Manuel Rodriguez, both thirteen years old, were hanging out. Dom was their gang leader, their elder mentor who, at twenty-three years old, was a drug, and alcohol provider. Dom leaned over, opening the back door. "C'mon, get in, Dudes. We'll get a pizza."

Eduardo responded hesitantly, "I thought you were mad at us for the bad deal yesterday?"

"Yeah, I was but 'cause you guys got no money, I'm letting you off. I'll get it back somehow."

The boys got in. They wore baggy oversized gangwear trousers and sleeveless T-shirts. Manuel laughed. "My mom thinks I'm in school. She's working today."

"Me, too," Eduardo added, "Who needs school? What are we going to do, become doctors?" They laughed together, thin immature voices, not yet soaked in testosterone, with Dom joining. Then they drove away from the shopping area on the freeway to the Badlands, on the edge of town. The highway wound and turned through earthquake escarpments and barren hills.

"I thought we were going for a pizza?" Eduardo asked.

"I wanna show you guys something first. Ever seen a eagles nest?"

"Naw, there's no eagles here." Manuel responded.

Dom added, "Sure, they up in the hills. The government hides them 'cause they endangered species."

Manuel wasn't convinced, "Well, I never seen 'em."

"Me neither," Eduardo said

They turned off on Jackrabbit Trail, a dirt road leading from the hills into the desert. After several turns between the hills, Dom stopped the car and turned the engine off. They all got out. Dom took the snub-nosed Rossi out of his pocket. He stood in front of Eduardo.

"I lied," Dom confessed. "You guys fucked me out of my twenty dollars for the check you stole from me yesterday! Nobody fucks with me!"

"No, man!" Eduardo replied, nervously staring at the gun. "Put that thing down. I'll get money from my mother."

Manuel began crying as Dom fired point blank at Eduardo, smiling strangely as he pulled the trigger three times. Eduardo fell back from the shock of the bullets, with a surprised expression on his face. Manuel turned, ran from the car. Dom fired again, hitting him in the back. The hammer clicked on spent caps as Manuel staggered over a rise, and fell out of sight.

"I'll come back and kill you!" Dom yelled. "I'm going for more ammo, motherfucker!" He drove away.

A dirt biker heard three rapid shots, BLAM, BLAM, BLAM, and then another, BLAM, as he gunned his Yamaha down a hill, flying over the crest of the next rise. "Yahoo!" he cried with excitement as the bike defied gravity for a moment, and then crashed down. Then he turned down a fork in the trail toward the sound where he encountered a teenager lying on the trail, wounded and coughing blood. A dust plume rose in the distance from Dom's car. The biker followed the dust, swerved around another teenager lying on the trail, but the car turned out of sight on the freeway. The biker continued to the corner of the freeway where he found a phone at a business, dialed 911. "There's two kids murdered!" He screamed at the operator.

"Where are you?" she calmly asked.

"Jackrabbit Trail in the Badlands."

"Your name, please and tell me what happened and we'll have a unit out there, pronto."

Five minutes later he was ushering a California Highway motorcycle officer off the freeway and led him to the murder scene. Seven black turkey vultures circled lazily in the sky overhead in a cone-shaped formation, marking the place for them. A year later, the biker would receive a letter of commendation from the Sheriff's Department for saving Manuel's life by his quick action.

Detective Nelson met with a deputy sheriff in a conference room of the County Sheriff's station in Badlands. They poured cups of coffee from the pot on the side table. "What do we have with this guy, Dom?" Nelson asked the deputy.

"Section 187 murder and intent to murder. Two Hispanic teenagers. Shot them in cold blood."

"This guy told you he worked for COLA radio?"

"Uh, huh. Works for Raymond McDade."

Nelson smiled, "You've made my day. Sounds like special circumstances." He knew the multiple murders of Tom and Eduardo would give him some leverage with Dom. Now he could focus on Raymond McDade.

"Sure. Death penalty… that is, solitary on death row, with the best of the well-paid Bar Association at taxpayer's expense." He paused. "Say, this guy Dom is a basket case. We kept him up all night… He's pretty worn down. He confessed to the boy's shooting. This guy is so fucked up I don't know how he ever held down a job with COLA or even a gas station."

"Good. Bring him to me." Nelson poured them both another cup of coffee.

They went into another room. The deputy tested a tape recorder. Dom was led in wearing an orange jump suit decorated with handcuffs, waist chain and leg irons connected in front with a keyed quick release box. He was fatigued, limp, belligerent, and had a blank, dense look in his eyes. His appointed defense lawyer was present. Nelson turned the tape recorder on and began. "Today is May 30, 1991. I'm Detective Nelson and am interviewing Domingo Malichera at the Badlands Sheriff's substation. Good morning, Mr. Malichera"

"Fuck you," Dom said.

Nelson read him his rights, had his counsel identify his presence, and continued. "Please answer the questions. Do you work for Raymond McDade at COLA radio?"

"Yeah."

"What do you do there?"

Dom proudly answered, "I'm an engineer. Made sure the station works all the time."

"What hours do you work?"

"Graveyard." Dom laughed.

"Did you ever meet a man named Tom Winters?"

"Naw, never heard of him. Can I have a cig?"

A cigarette was produced and lit. Nelson leaned forward. "Where were you on Tuesday, February the 19th?"

"I don't remember, man." Dom was trying hard not to look into Nelson's eyes.

"That was only yesterday."

"I don't remember. I think I was drunk all day."

The deputy appeared in the doorway, motioned for Nelson to break it off. Dom was left in the room with another deputy. "We just got a break," the deputy told Nelson. They found Tom Winters' stereo and television at Dom's apartment."

"Find the gun?"

"Not yet."

Nelson sighed in relief. "Now we have them all except for the murder weapon." He returned. "Mr. Malichera." Dom deliberately looked away. He was smoking a fresh cigarette from the other deputy. "Mr. Malichera," Nelson continued. "May I have your attention, please?" Dom gave him an, 'I don't care look'. "We know you killed Tom Winters. Now, why don't you just tell us about it and save a lot of time?"

"Why should I? What's in it for me? I don't believe you." He stubbed his fresh cigarette.

Nelson decided to end his polite role. "Confess, Dom! Get it over with! I have until retirement to get it out of you. You'll be here every single day until you die of old age. We have evidence you killed Tom Winters. How much did Raymond McDade pay you?"

Dom's counsel protested but Dom's defense collapsed. He coughed and looked down at the table. "He paid me $5,000." Dom stated with a sigh of relief as he looked up at the door.

Nelson hoped his nervousness didn't show. He remained cool although he wanted to shout out loud with excitement. "By check or cash?"

"Cash and two $500 checks. Supposed to be a robbery."

"Where's the gun?"

"At the station, Man."

"Where in the station?"

"The store room. My backpack is there. Ray gave me a key."

"Now, do you realize that what you said was of your own free will?"

"Yeah, man. I need to go to the bathroom." Dom suddenly broke down crying and mumbling incoherently about his mother and childhood. When his mental defenses were weakest, childhood memories about his family flooded out current awareness and reason. Nelson shut the recording machine off and broke away to make a call to the District Attorney's office. A lawyer was connected.

Nelson rejoined the deputy outside the room after he returned Dom with chains dragging from the men's room to the soundproofed interview room.

"Where are we with this guy?" the Deputy asked.

"The D.A. wants to send their guy to get something in writing. They'll probably offer a plea bargain later on for his cooperation. After all, it's Murder One with special circumstances."

"Good deal for this asshole. Life without parole instead of death row. He might wish he had the death sentence after fifty years in jail, if he isn't killed by then. I'll send him back to Woodland as soon as I get the release. Lunch, buddy? There's a truck stop nearby."

"Sure, oh hell, all your Badlands restaurants are truck stops." They laughed and Nelson continued; "now we get to break down the doors of Raymond McDade's mansion and the radio station. They're going to the judge for search warrants."

"What a fucking shame." The deputy was shocked by the cheapness of life in the hands of the man with a gun.

"Tom Winters? Killing the guy everybody loved?" Nelson remembered meeting with Tom's ex wife, kids and father; all deeply touched for a lifetime from the murder. He painfully observed the collateral damage from a senseless crime touching and breaking a web of innocent victims. He knew every man is capable of creating his own war zone of innocent casualties when there is no God or law they respect. He would go to church Sundays putting on the face with his family, knowing justice, the righteous arm of Godliness, was found here in this old cement block police station wearing uniforms and badges, not singing gospel. "They keep us in business. This dirty fucking business."

21
Rebirth Of Ronald Alwin May 31, 1991

Loud knocking on the front door woke Ray. He turned the light on, looked at his bedside clock. It was 4 A.M. "Who the hell is that?" he asked Alice as he got out of bed.

The noise continued. He put his robe on over his shorts, hurried downstairs. At the front door a lawyer from the District Attorney's office handed him a search warrant, pushed past him with several Police officers and plainclothes detectives. They fanned out and noisily went through cabinet drawers and a desk in the downstairs den. Alice, wearing pajamas, arrived at the top of the stairs, screaming in terror!

Detective Nelson appeared at the bottom of the stairs. "It's okay Ma'am. We have a warrant. Please go back to the bedroom and get dressed." She disappeared into the bedroom and locked the door.

A voice rose from the den, "Hey, there's a computer here. What do we do with it?" the officer asked.

The lawyer said, "I'll have to call the D.A., but it's too early. Let's save it for later." They continued tearing through the rooms with Ray standing in the kitchen shaking as he read and reread the warrant.

Hours later, after searching the rest of the house, the grounds, the huge garage with Ray's father awakened in his adjoining apartment, and all the cars, they had very little material for their work, mostly documents from Ray's den. It was obvious that Ray was not running his business from his house and that everything would be found at the radio station. At 8 A.M. the attorney present with the Police called the D.A.'s office about the computer he found in the den. A lawyer answered.

"I don't know anything about computers," the investigating attorney said. "How do I get into it?"

"Bring it in." The lawyer in the District Attorney's office said. They talked further. When he finished, he asked an officer go to the den to pick the machine up.

Alice, who was near the den, screamed at him, "My kid's homework is on the computer! You can't take it!"

"Sorry, Ma'am, we need it for evidence."

"Ray," Alice screamed, "Do something!" Ray shrugged helplessly.

"Mr. McDade, I need the keys to the business. The warrant covers it." Nelson had his hand out.

Ray went upstairs to the bedroom where an officer was searching, returned with a key ring with only one key on it. He handed it to the detective. "The studio is always open, you can go right in."

Nelson was not fooled. "No, we need all the keys to the rooms there. Otherwise we'll be breaking doors down and you wouldn't want that, would you?"

Ray took the 'do not duplicate' master key off another key ring from his pocket and handed it over. "This key fits all the doors. I'll go over with you."

"No need to. We prefer that you stay here." He turned to Alice, 'We're finished here, now. Bye, Ma'am." Looking up at Alice on the stairs, he nodded and left. *How could she be staying in the same bedroom with the guy who murdered her lover?* he thought.

Afterward Raymond took the tape recorder out from under the bed. He was surprised the Police missed it. He listened to the conversation between Detective Nelson and the DA lawyer. "What do we do with the computer? Nobody knows how to get inside it?" Nelson asked. "Bring it in," the lawyer responded. "By the way," he said, "Now that Dom confessed I bet Lucas Carranza sandbags this one." Nelson added, "Wouldn't surprise me. We're going to the business now. I'll keep you in touch."

Alice overheard the tape. An astonished look came over her face. "Dom did it? You had Dom killed my Tom?" she screamed hysterically.

"No! No! I told Dom not to do it. He offered to do it and I told him not to."

"You're lying!" Alice sobbed. "I don't believe you!"

Ray's face was red with embarrassment as he feigned anger. "You've got to believe me. We talked about it. He came to me and offered to do it. I changed my mind." Ray went to a closet, started packing a bag. "I've got to get out of here. They'll blame me for it."

Alice sat down on the bed, stared at the floor. "I don't believe this is happening to me! Oh Lord!"

Ray raced out of the bedroom, tripping down the brick stairway. For the first time he was scared, even more so than the day the Police interrogated him. Somehow he kept his chin up and lied his way through but this was something different. They were invading his home and business to put him away. He began shaking again. Everything was now up in the air. *Maybe I should have not killed the bastard,* he thought. *Maybe I should have killed Alice instead. With my money I could always get another woman.* He shouted back, "I'll get back to you after things cool off!"

Alice was left sobbing on the bed. John was standing cool and collected; Josh was in tears next to his mother.

That afternoon Detective Nelson rushed into the Woodland Police squad room. He held a plastic zip lock bag in the air. Carlson looked up from the boxes of paperwork he had been sorting through from the house search. The trophy in the bag was the stainless steel .38 caliber five round Rossi revolver. Nelson grinned from ear to ear. The bag label read COLA radio station, May 31, 1991. Carlson came over, slapped him on the back. ".... Took your time finding the gun for my guy Tom's bullet, didn't you? Is it still smoking?" He asked and everybody laughed.

"Better than that, I have hollow-point bullets and two different $500 checks made out to one Domingo Malichera."

"Now," Carlson announced, "We'll fry the McDade bastard. Call your lovely wife 'n let her know we'll be working late. It's party time!" They walked out together, but not before Carlson filled out a form and placed the gun and ammo into a small box, then a FedEx envelope addressed to the California Criminal Laboratory in Sacramento, California. It would be a week before they received the expected response.

Meanwhile, Ray disappeared, first to his mountain cabin, then to San Diego. He always loved San Diego which was about 100 miles from the office. The beautiful hotels and beaches were everywhere, even though he never had time to visit beyond a magazine or movie. One morning he rang the doorbell of a large old distinguished Victorian house. It was a solid house, well maintained; fish scale upper floor with white and blue gingerbread trim. He had a newspaper underarm, rang the door bell. A middle aged woman appeared. "Hi, I called about the room." He handed her his Mike Allen pseudonym COLA business card. Everybody in the station had a radio name to keep away from the public. "I'm here for a project we're doing on San Diego."

"I'll show you the room. There's no smoking, drugs, or drinking allowed here. I hope you don't have pets, either." She directed him upstairs to a large bedroom in the big rambling house. Ray was pleased and they agreed on the terms and rent. He paid her in cash and left.

The next morning Ray walked quickly down rows of tombstones to the Public Lot section of weathered grave markers which were not more than a steel washer with a name and dates driven into the gravesite with a spike. The San Diego morning fog made him uneasy. Seagulls cried overhead, distracting him. Using his shoe, he scraped the moss off the old markers of people too poor to afford a funeral or gravestone. He read the dates until he found Ronald Alwin, born and died February 18, 1943. Ray wrote on the back of a business card. *I'm suddenly going to be nine years younger,* he thought, smiling.

Ray visited the Central Library that afternoon. He sat at a large table in a room filled with research data periodicals, large heavy reference books, bound ledgers, and microfiche readers. Ray studiously sorted through the microfiche newspaper copies until he found what he came for under Obituaries, 'Gary A. Alwin, son of Lorena and Darrell Alwin, died one month after birth at the San Diego Community hospital yesterday, February 18th, 1943.' Ray copied the information on a business card and left, copiously thanking the clerk on the way out.

The next morning Ray completed a form at the City Bureau of Vital Statistics. He paid the $10 fee with an application listing Lorena and Darrell Alwin as his parents. He took a seat in the waiting room. Fifteen minutes later, the clerk handed him a copy of his new birth certificate. It was stamped CERTIFIED in purple ink with the city seal and the day's date.

That afternoon Ray, A. K. A. Ronald Alwin, after waiting in a line of elderly and disabled citizens, presented his birth certificate and paid a $15 fee for a new Social Security card. An hour afterward he pocketed the new card printed in blue and departed.

The following morning, Ronald Alwin, stood in several lines at the California Department of Motor Vehicles office and passed the written driving test after finding the exam booklet on a counter. He also passed the eye exam, had his picture taken, and made an appointment for the driving test, at the earliest, next week. No one noticed him driving away from the parking lot.

Later he found a job at the El Camino car wash to pass time. They paid cash tips daily and he happily wiped cars down for a week.

The next week he was handed the written grading form from the uniformed exam driver at the DMV. The tester congratulated him on passing the first time. Ronald Alwin could now drive. They would mail his driving license to his address nearby in San Diego.

Several weeks later when he arrived home from work, the middle-aged landlady was standing inside the foyer to confront him. "Who is Ronald Alwin?" she asked, agitated.

"Is there mail?" Ray ignored her question. "I'm expecting something from the DMV."

"For Ronald Alwin?"

"Yes, it's my other business name," Ray answered, holding his hand out for the letter which she reluctantly handed him.

"I want you to leave," she demanded. "I don't know what you're up to and I don't care. Please leave by next week. Do you understand?"

Ray nodded and headed upstairs to his room to look at the usual terrible photo on his driving license.

The next morning he called Alice from a public phone at the Mission Bay beach. He was overjoyed to hear her voice. "Alice, are you and the kids okay?"

"Ray, where have you been? Yeah, the kids are fine."

"Have the cops been by again?"

"No. Are you coming home?"

"Is it safe? I mean, they won't arrest me if I come by?"

"I don't know," she said dejectedly. "They tore the office up and took all kinds of papers and the computers. I don't know what's happening."

"Look, get the kids and meet me here at the Marina Hotel at Mission Bay beach outside San Diego at seven tonight. Bring me money and clothes, okay? I'm going to call you by your radio name Jennifer, from now on in case anybody is listening. Tell the kids in case they pick up the phone."

The machine informed Ray that it needed to be fed more change.

Alice sounded confused. "Ray, you know… I don't know what to think about what happened. I'm not sure I'm doing the right thing."

"Just remember that I love you. That's what counts, Honey. See you later." He hung up.

That evening Ray, Alice and the kids went to a park bench overlooking the Mission Bay. The cool evening air, a welcome relief from the Woodland summer heat, invigorated the boys who immediately took their tennis shoes off to run through the wet sand at the water's edge.

"How's the business going?" Ray asked.

"Bad. I brought one of our sales guys' back, Mitch's assistant Frank, to help me run it. The cash flow is terrible. We had a hell of a time getting the computers with the billing back from the Police." She vacantly watched the boys on the beach. "Ray, I'm terribly tired. This whole thing and the business are unreal." She handed him a wad of $100 bills which he stuffed in his pants pocket as he looked around nervously.

He grabbed both of her hands. "I've got to leave."

"Maybe I can rent a house for you to stay until this thing cools down."

"Good idea. Do it right away. I've got to stay in a motel until then."

She got up and walked to the beach to collect the kids. Ray looked at the boys, surprised that John looked so much like him and was also quiet and observant, with long red hair, but taller. He called back, "I love you. I'll call every day. By the way, my landlady kicked me out." She stopped for him to finish, "My new name is Ronald Alwin."

The next week Alice supervised a move to an Indian Hills tract house. The movers trundled furniture back and forth. At the end of the day they finished and Alice paid them in cash. Ray happily moved about inside putting things away, humming to himself, but not venturing outside. Alice came inside, closing the front door for the last time. Ray approached her. "It's sure not like the mansion." They embraced like newlyweds.

"At least you have a place to stay."

"Correction, Lady, we have a place to stay. Now I can help you with the business…
from here."

Alice was worried. "This was awkward with me quitting school, leaving my
Mother and Pops to take care of the kids. We should be taking care of them. When
will this end?"

"Someday. We still have each other."

"Do you think the owner believed you were my brother?"

"Who knows? I think he just wanted the ten grand for the lease option."

A week later after lunch, Ray saw and heard about the murder on the television news.
The suspect had fled, the news clip concluded after showing a gruesome murder scene
with blood-spattered walls, sofa and carpets. Suddenly, Ray felt painful pressure inside
his chest and through his back. The angina increased as Ray panicked. He broke into
a sweat, thinking about the two mild prior heart attacks. *Maybe this is the big one,* he
thought, as he shut the television off. The discomfort gradually went away. Ray was
afraid to check in at the hospital. He went to the medicine cabinet and found the
nitroglycerine prescription bottle empty. *Thank God it still has refills,* he thought as
he called Alice. *I'll have to establish a diet and exercise program to get back in shape,* he
decided while Alice was at the drug store. Fortunately, the clerk didn't recognize his
name. She brought the prescription home with the usual huge box of paperwork for
him to work on. One thing he couldn't get rid of was the stress.

Later after he settled down, Alice asked, "Ray, do you have a life insurance
policy?"

"No, Honey."

"Then you need to get one. Don't you think?"

"Too late. I'm a fugitive from justice and medically don't qualify. We don't need
one because we have the business."

"I hope it gets better."

He ignored the signs and the next day ordered lumber to build an addition to the
house to make more room for Pops. The mansion was empty and listed for sale. Alice
would know where to find Ray when the sales documents needed to be signed.

On June 24, 1991, Detective Nelson visited the Budget Rental Car office on University
Avenue in Woodland. He had a Master Card receipt for a car rental dated February
19, 2001. He showed his badge and then the receipt to the clerk. "Do you remember
renting a car to Raymond McDade on this date?" he asked. The clerk nodded no.
"Then would you please give me a photocopy of the car rental documents for this deal?"
The rental clerk went to a file drawer and produced the rental form, copied it and gave
Nelson the copy. "Thanks a lot." Nelson said smiling as he saw Ray's driver's license on

it. *Now, why would a guy need to rent a car on the murder night when he has 14 cars of his own?* He thought as he went back to the station. *I wonder what his alibi will be?*

That afternoon Nelson called Lucas Carranza at the District Attorney's office. "Luke, where do we stand on the McDade case?" he asked. There is no shortage of evidence on him."

"Hang on to your hat, partner. I'll be going for an indictment and Grand Jury soon. Meanwhile, find out where McDade is. We will need him afterward." Lucas laughed over the phone, "It's going to be collection time at the OK Corral."

Several days later Ray answered the phone from the tract house in Indian Hills. "Ray, the police called and wanted to know where to find you. They said I could be an accomplice if I don't tell them. I think they want to arrest you."

"What did you tell them?" He asked nervously.

"I didn't know where you were. I'm worried." Her voice was trembling with fear.

"Don't tell them anything!" Ray ordered. "Don't do anything suspicious like leaving early or calling again." Ray went to the bureau drawer, digging under sheets until he found a flat cookie tin. Opening it, he gazed at his fabulous collection of rare uncirculated American gold coins, all graded and sealed in individual packets. *I'll need them for cash,* he thought as he placed them in his suitcase and began packing.

When Alice came home that evening there was a note from Ray. "Alice, the car [Lincoln] is in Ontario airport. You should be able to find it. I'm sorry; I don't know what to do. I did not do anything wrong. No one believes me, even you! I'll send you something in the mail. Tell the boys & I love them very much. Take care of yourself & things. Ray."

Ray, like the person driving faster when the gas tank is near empty, was on a long trip to nowhere.

22

Aloha, June 25, 1991

Richard Hussack was all smiles, tanned, slim, wearing shorts and a colorful Hawaiian Tommy Bahamas floral silk shirt as he greeted Ray. "Goddamn, Ray! I never expected to see you here. You're lucky I was home when you called from the airport."

They embraced. "I was in a hurry. Marital problems." Ray said.

Richard picked up one of the bags. "Well, we all have that from time to time, pal." They walked to the Jeep.

"I thought I could help get the new station started and cool it for a while. I'll be able to see how some of the used equipment I sent you is working."

"You're welcome any time. Matter of fact, I'm going to the mainland soon and you can have the place all to yourself. Afterward, you can help me finish the start-up." They drove away, chattering old buddies.

On July 4th Alice joined Ray for a Maui vacation. One morning, two days later, they enjoyed a fabulous brunch with a huge spread of fish, fruit and vegetables at a resort restaurant. Later, they were drinking strong Kona coffee outside watching the boys swimming. As expected, the conversation reverted to business as Alice informed Ray about the station. "Jack Clafner, your old partner, says he has venture capital people in San Francisco to buy the business."

"Jesus, Alice, of all people. Anybody else interested?" Ray's disgust was evident.

"Just a bunch of callers. Maybe Jack is the best bet. He says the sale price of $30 million is way too high because the business is doing so badly."

"Jack will steal us blind first. I don't trust him." Ray remembered the constant fighting between them with Jack always trying to wheedle the station away from Ray after it began to make money. Ray did all the work; Jack talked about it and took the profits.

Alice gazed hypnotically at the calming beach and ocean. "This place is heaven. Why couldn't we do this before?" Ray looked at her blankly. "Vacations, like other people."

"The business never sleeps, that's why," he answered coldly.

"The business that kills people." Alice replied.

"I need more money."

"The business is broke. I put our payroll on a payroll service and they charge us for the taxes when we write the checks. We can't fudge on the deposits any more. The accountant told me to do it so I can keep it straight. He said you micromanaged everything, but I can't handle the payroll without help."

"There's more cash in the locked filing cabinet in the storage room. A sealed envelope marked tax records."

"How much is there?"

"$37,000. Wire me $10,000 right away to Ronald Alwin."

"That's incredible! I never knew you had a stash!"

Ray smiled, "It was from the concert promotion. Now you know my last secret."

"Well," Alice said, "you sure know all of mine."

On a hot humid early August day, Ray filled out the DSP-11 passport form, paid a fee, gave the postal clerk the Ronald Alwin birth certificate and two photos. The clerk held up his hand to swear him in. "Do you solemnly swear that the information is correct to the best of your knowledge? If so, please sign." He pointed to the signature line on the form.

"I do. How long will it take?"

"It goes to Honolulu. Up to a month, Mr. Alwin."

"Thanks, I'll be in touch."

"We'll deliver," smiled the clerk, "come rain or shine, remember?"

"Right, bye." Ray stepped outside into the warm rain.

Back at the station Nate Perkins was doing his noon news broadcast. He read from his morning script. "There is no news on the whereabouts of Raymond McDade, the missing murder suspect who owns this radio station and was my employer. An all points bulletin for his arrest has been issued by the Woodland Police Department. Mr..."

The sound room door suddenly burst opened. Alice tore through, screaming. "Cut it off Nate! No more about Ray! Do you hear?"

Nate was appalled that he had been interrupted on the air. "Excuse me folks," he told his audience, "I'll be right back with more news." He cut the mike, motioned to the engineer on the other side of the window. *Build Me Up Buttercup* by the Foundations music resumed overhead. Nate rushed out of the sound room. Alice was nowhere to be seen.

About the same time Ray clipped a newspaper article, 'Brazilian man acquitted of killing wife and lover in Defense of Honor.' The article suggested that although it was not part of the legal code, the South American barbaric defense was solemnly accepted by the courts. Ray called a local travel agency for travel brochures on South America. *Argentina doesn't have an extradition treaty,* he thought, as he made sure to ask especially for Argentina travel information.

The computer operator at the State Department of Diplomatic Security, officially known as the Passport and Visa Screening Department, input the application for Ronald Alwin. The computer blinked as it accepted the data for comparison and filing. Suddenly a warning flashed on the screen: DECEASED APPLICANT. The clerk then printed out data from the screen, took it and the application to her supervisor for immediate review.

"Thanks, Jackie," she said, "Another phony. Please copy and FedEx to the Agent in Charge at the Los Angeles office.

The clerk stamped the FedEx envelope: JOHN DOE INFANT DEATH INVESTIGATION, and sent it on the way.

The following week Victor Smith, the Assistant Agent in Charge of the Los Angeles office, received the Ronald Alwin application from the Washington Section Chief. He reviewed the data, gave the file to his secretary. Then he called Honolulu. "I've got a phony application from the Maui Post office. Want to visit him?"

"Can you handle it? My traveling guy is on vacation?"

"Hell, you guys are always on vacation in Hawaii. I need a vacation, too. I'll schedule somebody your way for next week. Meanwhile, I'll fax you the application and you can get more information from this guy."

"Okay, I'll send out the supplemental to hang him up. I don't think he will be leaving without his passport."

"By the way, where do Hawaiians go on vacation?"

"When it gets hot and humid in the late summer, we all go back to the states to visit relatives."

Several weeks later Ray received a SUPPLEMENTAL INFORMATION FORM from the Honolulu passport office. Ray completed the form and enclosed photocopies of Alwin's Social Security card, San Diego Driving License, and a business card showing him as station manager of Hussack's radio station. There was also a manila envelope from Jack Clafner of San Francisco. Ray opened it to find Woodland Press clippings of Tom's murder and an article showing Ray as a missing suspect.

John received an evening call from Ray to the Indian Hills house. He ran for his mother. "Mom, its Dad!" he cried with excitement.

Alice took the phone, "What now, Ray! I just had a hell of a day at the office."

"Jennifer, I'm coming home!"

"What? You're crazy. The police are looking for you. They think you left the country."

"My passport application is hung up in Los Angeles. I have to untangle it."

"What do you want with a passport?"

"I'm going to Argentina. We can sell the business and live like kings there. The kids'll love it. How are they doing in school?"

"This neighborhood is terrible. They fight with other kids every day here. I can't take this life and the business any more. Your son John has a black eye. It's crazy!"

"Hang on. I'm coming in on flight 235 from Honolulu on Hawaiian Airlines. I'll meet you in LAX on arrival, September 17. Write it down … okay?"

"No, it's not okay. I'm tired Ray, just worn out."

"Hang in there, Honey. Just meet me at the airport. I'll see you, bye"

Alice fished through her purse for the card she thought she would never need. "Detective Nelson, please."

"Hello?"

"Detective Nelson, I'm sorry to bother you at this hour."

"Is this Alice McDade?"

"Sorry, I'm a bundle of nerves, that's why I had to call you."

"It's okay. Now, what's your problem? Is Ray back in town?"

"Ray's in Hawaii. He'll be leaving on Hawaiian Airlines flight 235 on 9/17 from Honolulu. He wants me to meet him at LAX."

"Thanks, Ma'am. I appreciate the tip," Nelson said. "Are you okay? You don't sound good. I'm glad you aren't hiding him. That would make you an accomplice."

"I'm worn out. This has to end," she paused. By the way, he's using the name Ronald Alwin."

Ray's flight was on time. He was standing in line when a man wearing a dark suit unlike the sport shirted and shorts travelers, accompanied by a Maui policeman, approached him. "Raymond McDade, you're under arrest. Please place your hands behind you."

"You've got the wrong man. I'm Ronald Alwin," Ray said.

"We know." Detective Nelson answered. "We know all about it. I'm going to read you your rights."

Detective Nelson recited the Miranda Rights from memory as they cuffed him and hustled him off to an airport office for booking and his defense lawyer call. The Maui police officer stayed behind asking the airline counter clerk to hold up the flight and offload Ray's baggage from the L-1011 jet. She called into the phone and ran to the pilot in the cockpit to stop the flight.

The next day Ray and Nelson left handcuffed together on another flight to Los Angeles. Ray's lawyer, in suit, saddleback shoes, and bowtie, left little encouragement and departed on a later flight. The luggage search revealed travel information and plane tickets to Argentina from LAX.

Special Agent Victor Smith and plainclothes Sergeant Bianca huddled with the Maui Post Office clerk in the back room. The flip calendar showed the date, September 18, 1991. The Special Agent produced a composite of six photographs. The clerk pointed to Ray. "That's him."

"Sure?"

"I remember him because he was so nervous."

"Thanks." He turned to the Sergeant. "Let's arrest Ronald Alwin or whoever he is."

"Yes Sir." The Sergeant patted his shoulder holster.

They got directions from the clerk and drove to the Hussack condo. Nobody answered the bell. A neighbor walked by, stopped.

"Looking for Mr. Alwin?" she asked.

"Yes, Ma'am," the Agent said.

"He left with his stuff yesterday."

"Say where he was heading for?" the Sergeant said.

"No Sir. Very quiet fellow. Just left with his bag."

The Agent looked at his companion and answered. "Thanks Ma'am. You've been a great help"

After unsuccessfully trying their cell phone, they hurried to use a telephone at the Post Office. "Shit, he got away," the Agent reported to Los Angeles. Let's put out an all-points-alert to pick up Ronald Alwin."

"Seemed like a smart guy." The postal clerk added.

As Raymond and Nelson flew to Los Angeles there were no words spoken, the result of a discussion between Ray and Brian Newman, his criminal attorney. Ray's hands trembled uncontrollably. The silence became a stupor. For the first time in his life Ray was terrified and didn't have a solution for an immediate problem; his life was out of control.

23

Incarceration

Walter Davis was penciling out a corporate tax return when the phone rang with Ray's daily collect call. "Walt, you have to visit," Ray pleaded. "We need to go over the sale deal." His voice reflected the unthinkable, life in the county jail for a millionaire who once controlled every aspect of his life and other people. "It's terrible here. You've got to help get me out. I didn't do it."

"Okay, Ray. I'll visit as soon as I can. What are the hours?"

"Visiting time is from six to seven P.M. I'm in the jail at the back of the old courthouse, but you need to go to the new jail across the street first. Bye." The phone disconnected. Walt remembered the jail behind the courthouse. Once he went downstairs into the dark stale dungeon where wire covered lights hung from concrete ceilings to fingerprint for a National Association of Security Dealers application. The butch female Deputy looked at him as if he was a serial killer. *Everyone besides Deputies were outsiders… kinda like being a criminal,* he thought at the time.

He remembered the attitude several days later as he checked in at the jail in the new courthouse. Outside the new courthouse entrance was a large plaza with a solidly built trellis with concrete posts suitable for a public hanging. He was ushered across the street with a gaggle of polyester-dressed Hispanics and black people, some with children. They were herded into a dimly lit windowless tomb, a far cry from the Grecian-columned courthouse viewed by the public on the opposite side of the block. There was heaviness to the cement floors, walls, and stairs which reminded Walt of German bunkers and pill boxes from his time in Europe. A shiver went back his back leaving him uncomfortable. He entered an elevator, went up several flights and out into another chamber where a Deputy behind a thick window and through a microphone, called out, "Everybody leave all notebooks and purses on the floor."

They waited. A smiling Hispanic man with many Bibles under his arm was given preference and taken inside. Religion appeared to be an easy ticket into the place, but maybe not out. Walt felt uneasy being entombed in the dark damp place where body smells and sweat never left. It reminded him of a Nazi SS interrogation building in the Hartz Mountains that also smelled of urine, but this seemed worse since it had aged. Here, the swastikas were missing from the posts on either side of the steel gated high stone walls. Walter was finally admitted through steel doors to a large room filled with a rounded riveted steel structure punctured by small glass porthole windows, strangely reminiscent of a ship. A telephone was hanging outside each window.

Ray filed into the chamber with other prisoners wearing orange jumpsuits. His toupee was missing making him appear much older. Large circles surrounded tired brown eyes. He had lost weight and his skin was even paler than from the sunless office of his radio station domain. Walt picked up the phone outside Ray's window to welcome him.

"Walt, I'm so glad to see you!" Ray exclaimed. The static was bad.

"I can hardly hear you," Walt said. "You sound a thousand miles away."

"The line goes through a tape recorder," Ray said. "Walt, my attorney isn't doing anything for me. He doesn't even visit. I need to get out so I can work on the radio station sale and my case. I didn't kill Tom Winters." I'm going crazy here."

"I don't know what to say, Ray." I haven't talked to your lawyer. The only people contacting me are Alice and some calls about the business sale."

"You've got to get me out of here. Help me sell the real estate, business, anything."

"Jack Clafner called the other day from San Francisco with a phony deal for you on the sale. Claims he can get you cash for the station in a tax-free stock swap. Must have invented new tax code rules."

"Walt, my brain is turning to mush here. Watch out for Jack. He'll do anything to get the station. You'll have to sort through my finances until the situation is over." Ray stared vacantly into the inch-thick glass porthole. "This place has terrible food, three holding tanks of forty people each and overcrowding with people sleeping on the floors. They wake us up at four or five A.M. for gravy hamburger on toast-SOS, the prisoners call it, with a hard boiled egg and milk. Lunch is rotten food. Dinner is green rotten pork with spaghetti or Mexican food. We have to chew our nails off." He held up bloody fingers. "Nail clippers not allowed. Exercise is up on the roof. I share my six by nine cell with two other inmates. Yesterday, we had a harassment roll call and had to stand by the beds while a prisoner, who badmouthed a guard, was beaten with a baton. Mexican TV channel every other night in the hallway, black channel other nights."

A Hispanic lady held a squirming baby up to an opposite window for her prisoner-husband to see. The prisoner placed his hand on the window.

"My attorney should be getting me out on bail but nothing's happening." Ray kept rubbing irritating beard stubble. I was carded and lost television rights for losing my id bracelet which fell off because I lost weight."

"Don't they let you shave here?" Walt asked.

You wouldn't believe it. One Bic razor for all forty people. It gets so dull that your face breaks out. We have to shave using the chrome plate at the telephone for a mirror. They card you for anything at all."

"Jesus, Ray, this is more like a concentration camp."

"I'm the oldest prisoner. I told them I was here on drugs because everybody else is. Now I cut their hair with old razors. I'm the prison barber. We're all guilty by arrest. Get me some magazines. I need to put them under the mattress so I don't get the bed springs in my back. The phone suddenly went dead. Walt waved back to Ray as he was herded out."

The receptionist held two cowboys from Badlands at bay in Walt's waiting room. They were admiring the wall of leather bound tax-legal books which lined a wall of the spacious main room with floor-to-ceiling book cases.

Walt cleared his desk and admitted them to his private office. One cowboy, wearing a big hat, boots, and grin, offered a large 100 page letter-sized bound book proudly to Walt. "Here you go partner, a $15 million dollar offer for COLA from the 'Burner' station in Badlands. You can't beat that!"

"Let's go to lunch and discuss it." It'll take days to digest the deal before I get back to Ray." Walt hefted the book, started leafing through it.

"Sure partner, we brought the limousine." The cowboys clomped out of the office, hard leather heels on hardwood floors, to a rental limousine at the curb." They lunched at the Sheraton Hotel while filling Walt's ears with wondrous tales of radio station management as he skimmed through the offer. Later as they parted company, Walt wondered where they were really coming from. Badlands is where cowboys and coyotes live in harmony, not the big money for radio station COLA. He spent the rest of the afternoon studying the documents.

Brian Newman, Ray's impeccably dressed criminal defense attorney, was ushered into the sparse office of Lucas Carranza in the huge County building. The little office was crammed with bookcases piled with opened books, bound and unbound documents, papers everywhere from legal-sized files. It strangely resembled Ray's little office. It was obvious to Brian that the successful prosecutor was not in the business of impressing people; he was a doer… a hands-on non-delegater person who immersed himself in the details of his cases. They shook hands. Lucas, the sturdy dark haired, bright sharp-eyed man who could have passed for an unobtrusive accountant or doctor, but who could present a flawless case in court, wore a short sleeved white shirt, a colorful polyester birthday present tie folded on the book shelf behind him. "So you represent Raymond McDade?" Lucas asked.

"Yes," Brian answered.

"Well, that guy is in trouble. You can't get him bail because he has a prior conviction with three years probation and he also fled the area before we could arrest him. A very violent guy, your Raymond McDade. We have a zillion people who overheard or even participated in McDade's murderous rage. We have the smoking gun and a confession by the murderer. An open and shut case." He waited for the inevitable plea bargain offer.

"I want to save the County and my client a million dollars of court costs," Brian said. "I personally don't think my case is winnable without a big fight."

Lucas leaned forward, "With all respects Brian, I don't think he belongs on the street. I think we should convict him and throw away the key to his jail cell. I know I can get a conviction of murder one, along with kidnapping and other items." He paused, "Brian, this guy could get outside and do it again!"

"Can the County afford another big trial? You also have the William Lester Suff serial murderer to contend with and that will be a media event as well."

Lucas weighed matters. He knew the case would force a huge investigation, immense travel costs, and could tie the court up for a month or more. Worse, it would fall on him to prosecute and that would require months of late-night preparation and attention from him. The demands of his job always fall heavily on his family, leaving him unable to plan events or find time off. He was a perfectionist; unable to avoid details which could make the difference between winning or losing a case; unable to escape the demands he put on himself to leave no avenue open for technical error or holes in his prosecution. He had never lost a case, either. "I'll talk to the D. A., to see if I can get charges reduced to second degree murder for you. Personally, I can win it without the bargain. I really don't want this guy back on the street but I'll present your offer to the Chief as a workload issue although I don't agree. We'll see what the big guy wants."

"The fifteen year mandatory sentence would be okay with me if you drop the other charges. I'll talk to my client." Brian smiled. He could get what he wanted. All he had to do was convince his client and keep his $38,000 retainer. With time off for good behavior Ray would be out in 7-½ years, even less with time already served. They shook hands and he left to visit his client with the possible good news.

Later that day, Ray made his perfunctory afternoon collect call to his accountant. Walt told him about the big $15,000,000 offer from the cowboys. "Send it to me. I'll go over it," Ray said.

"Sure, but a word of caution, Ray. I looked at it and there's no substance."

"What do you mean?"

"No cash. No big down payment. Just unlisted stocks shown as assets for collateral. No company, either, just a Los Angles lawyer. I think it's a sham. They could get the deal hung up and find another buyer with serious money."

"Send it. Be sure to take any binders off it or they'll send it back. Dangerous weapons stuff. Jack visited and wants to make a deal with me. I have to see all deals," he insisted. "By the way, my attorney wants me to plea bargain and have me plead guilty." I didn't do it, Walt."

"You're going to turn him down? Go for a trial?"

"I'm not guilty, Walt. I can't agree for something I didn't do. Jack Clafner is going to find me a better trial lawyer. He's on the phone calling all over Beverly Hills for me."

Walt's appointment was standing in his doorway. "Well, Ray, I've got to go. Good luck with your case." I'll send the documents. Bye." Walt hadn't been paid in a long time and the radio station sale was beginning to consume all of his time.

Alice visited Ray with the children. They were nervous and fidgety but glad to see their father again. There was fear in their eyes and they clung to Alice as they kept looking around the concrete bunker. John took the phone first. "I miss you, son. Next Tuesday I've got a bail bond hearing and I want you to have your mother gas the car up and have it ready for me. I'm getting out of here. Can you do that?" John nodded yes.

Alice took the phone as John stepped aside. Josh reached for the phone but was pushed aside. "I want the divorce settled," she said.

"I'm going to make it clear, Honey that you won't see any money from the station if you testify against me in court."

"I'm the main witness. I can't lie to save you, Tom's murderer. Not for love or money." She hung up.

"Mommy, why are you crying?" Josh said.

"It's nothing. I just don't feel good when I come to this place."

"I don't want to come back, ever," John said. "I hate it here"

Ray had forgotten his father's rule of not speaking out loud about business. His father would have put a hand over his mouth, while shaking his head. Now Ray was all alone.

Lucas approached the District Attorney after the meeting with Brian. "I got a second degree murder bargain offer for McDade." Lucas said.

"Any way out for him?" The very tall executive said.

"No way out. Our detectives did a great job and we have our case. The only consideration is the cost of a big trial and tying our people up for the duration. "

"I say go ahead. Sometimes we need a big one to shock the public and shake the cobwebs out of the system."

"Okay, Chief. I don't want him to buy his way out of this one."

"We can use some good publicity, too."

"By the way Chief, are there any openings in the executive branch?"

"You're the best of the five hundred people in my office but I intend to live another fifty years and the Assistant District Attorney isn't going anywhere either. I created the Deputy Assistant position for you but there is nowhere else at the top. Besides, I would lose my best lawyer if you get promoted to my job. Maybe you could be our next Latino Senator or Congressman."

"Okay. I get the message. Thanks for the recommendation."

"By the way, Lucas, the William Lester Suff serial killer trial will be an interesting one. We have indications that he not only violently reduced the population of prostitutes along University Avenue, but that he may have also served chili made from some of them, for a barbeque with his co-workers."

"Yeah, I heard. Those guys in the City will eat anything. Maybe the stock clerk thought he was doing a new public service. Those poor girls are like weeds. Everybody pulls them up and they keep coming back. I'm glad to miss this case. I'll need a break after Ray's trial."

The D.A. opened the door. "I don't want Ray McDade coming back. Lock him up for life." They shook hands.

24

Extortion

Jack Clafner, a fast-talking sixty-year old man with a large waistline, filled the doorway in Walter Davis' office. Trailing two feet behind him was his acolyte, about ten years older and much thinner.

"Hi. I'm Jack Clafner, this is Herb Rosen. I've got a five million dollar deal for Raymond." They shook hands. A business card appeared and was handed to Walt.

"Let's see the deal," Walt.

"Can't disclose the details now."

"I just bounced a deal from the Badlands cowboys because it was all smoke. How do I know yours is any better?"

Jack produced a thin grey brochure from Murr, Reagan, Seleage & Company, a venture capital firm. "You'll have to trust me. We have mezzanine financing available from them when Ray and I strike the proper terms."

"Well, I'll tell Ray when he calls."

"No need to. I'm talking to him from here on. He'll be calling the radio station. Herb will be the new station manager. By the way, Ray turned down a fifteen-year plea bargain. I've got a better lawyer for him now."

"Another lawyer? The last one cost $38,000."

Jack shrugged. "I was lucky to get this guy. This one was in the famous Patti Hearst trial…the trial assistant from Chicago, Marty Tannenbaum."

"How can Ray afford him? We're trying to sell his real estate now."

"I have a Licensed Management Agreement with Herb to operate the station while Ray is…let's be kind and say 'indisposed.'" Jack smiled at Walt. "This way he can get some legal fees advanced."

"How much?"

"A million to start," Jack Said. "Plus we get $10,000 monthly to operate the station."

Walt shook his head. "What a mess."

"It's his own fault. All over that crazy wife. Guess who moved in with her? Bill Waters, that's who."

Walters look was poison. "Does that mean that Alice is out?"

"Obviously. She's living with Waters in the big house now."

"By the way," Walt added, "I had an agreement with Ray to get paid the $5,000 he owes me when a big federal tax refund arrives. Have you seen it yet?"

Herb Rosen stepped forward. "I'll have a look at it. As the new station manager I'll be in touch…especially since Alice won't be there any more."

Walt stood up, held his hand out. "Well, see to it then. Good day, gentlemen." They left.

Five minutes later, Walt's phone rang. "Did you hear what Ray and Jack put together?" Alice asked.

"Yes, the LMA deal. They just left. I feel like I just met Satan in a polo shirt. That guy reminded me of the Screaming Blue Meanie from the Yellow Submarine."

"Ray agreed to sell to them for five million. They're providing lawyers for the trial, too."

"Are you really out of the business?"

"Yeah, gladly. They're putting the company into receivership to keep it operating. Pops is living at the station for a while until I get another place. I'm staying with Bill Waters now because I'm still afraid of the other murderer out there. He could kill me because I'm a witness."

"This is a sorry mess. I feel sorry for you and the kids."

"Got to go. I'll get back. Bye."

Several months later Walt visited the station to talk with Herb. "Did you hear about the litigation?" Herb asked.

"What litigation?"

"I guess you didn't know. We got a fax at the office labeled 'PRESS RELEASE' from a publicity-seeking local husband and wife attorney team who are suing the station and Ray for thirty million with a wrongful death suit."

"A press release? Jesus, what's next? Can't they even wait until he's convicted? Well, I can't blame the Winters family for wanting revenge."

"Not Tom Winters. It's the Eduardo Sanchez kids' family. They say Ray provided the gun the kids were shot with. Lucky, Ray had Officers and Directors liability insurance," He paused, and then continued. "That's not all."

Walter was taking notes on a lined pad.

"Ray had to borrow against the office building and took a big down payment on the pending radio station sale. It all went to the lawyers."

They went to lunch and discussed the transition of the distressed business.

Alice called Walt several months later. "We can't sell the big house. The escrow folded because so much work was done out of code in the back. The bank won't finance the buyer unless it's brought up to code. I switched the pool filter pump timer to come on at night. That'll save a few dollars a month in utilities." Alice paused, "You know Walt, we're trying to sell a half-million dollar house and I have to save a few dollars on utilities to get by."

"Alice, what's left? What else can go wrong?"

"Mitch, the Gringo called to say hello. He's happy in Mexico with Nancy."

"Well, good for him. At least he got away from the rat race. I'll have to visit some day."

"Got to go now. Keep in touch, Walt. Bye."

Walt began thinking about Alice's life. *Now she was living with a guy who made minimum wages and has nothing going for him. He doubted that she needed the guy around for a bodyguard. Alice was still a fine looking woman, what a waste.* He picked up the beautiful black hawk statue from Mitch. He stroked it, thinking, *Mitch, you lucky devil, you've found Nirvana.*

Months passed with memos and calls flying back and forth from the new station manager, Herb Rosen, his partner Jack Clafner, the Court Receiver Maury Rosenfelder in Beverly Hills, and other lawyers. Ray no longer called Walt. One day, Walt's secretary led George Jackman to Walt's desk. The impeccably dressed, thin, handsome, black man about thirty-five, introduced himself. "I heard you were representing the COLA radio station sale." He handed a business card reading Media Brokers of Los Angeles.

"Well, Ray has other people handling most of his affairs these days. I'm his accountant. What can I do for you?"

"I represent people in Los Angeles who are interested in the station."

"You're not alone. We have two or three offers now, but it is under consideration. What do your people have?"

"I represent people with money. After all, I knew Jesse Johnson when he wore a leather jacket all the time. He learned how to wear a suit when I straightened him out."

"Do you represent Jesse or the NAACP?" Walt responded.

"Now, I'm not saying that," Jackman said. "Just that I know people with money."

"At any rate, you should get a proposal together and submit it. I'll get it to the right party."

"Okay. You'll hear from me. Thanks for the meeting. By the way, do you know of any other business opportunities?"

"Well, the real estate corporation next door is for sale. They have a huge net operating loss that might be useful to the right buyer. Ask for Jim."

"Thanks, I might drop in on my way out." They shook hands and parted.

A month later, Walter arrived at the COLA studio. The office was empty, strangely silent, and almost shut down. The banks of electronic equipment were missing; empty metal slots testified to their absence. Herb Rosen was in Ray's office. He handed Walt a bound letter-sized document as thick as a phone directory. "Here it is, Walt. The LMA agreement, the purchase offer from Jack Clafner's people, the letter of intent to purchase, and finally the deal book on the offer."

"How can things be so complicated?"

"This is big business now. I don't know how Ray did it alone. But that's not all." Herb's voice changed. "That's nothing. A guy named George Jackman tried to hang up the deal with extortion."

"You're kidding, Herb. The guy came by my office asking questions and I told him to see you guys if he had an offer."

"The guy demanded a piece of the action, board of director's spot, shares of stock, an interest in COLA... for nothing."

"For nothing?"

"Or he would litigate and appeal the radio station deal." Herb picked up a fax and handed it to Walt. The fax, from a Washington DC law firm, stated that a hand-written licensing violation complaint had been filed with the Federal Communications Commission by Jackman, acting as a friend of the court, stating that the station was unattended and unmanaged while Ray was away; that Alice, the station manager, was unlicensed, that the court receiver was wrongly appointed, and a list of other charges. After Walt read it, his face was devoid of color. "We squashed it with the LMA deal which showed it under management for the transition and the FCC trashed the complaint as frivolous."

"You know, Herb, its beginning to look like Ray was the nice guy in this business. Say, I'm on the mailing list from Jack in San Francisco and he has quite a sense of humor. Refers to the Ray and Alice 'dance' about their divorce. Says Ray lies like a rug about the murder. Is he some kind of comedian?"

"He thinks Ray screwed him when they were partners way back."

"Alice told me that Ray did all the work running the station and that Jack was never around until he was bought out. I also heard from a client that some equipment disappeared where Ray was working and that it may have gone to the new radio station when Ray and Jack started it up. I heard it was losing money until they took it over and changed the call letters." It appears that Ray was in bed with his enemy. What now? Where does the merry-go-round stop?"

"Well, I don't know what happened way back then. All I know is that the station was really out of business when we came in. They were operating on 1,000 watts back-up power, there were no sales and the receivables were all bad. We had to let everybody go. For your information, Ray signed over a power of attorney to the new lawyer in Century City handling the business sale and related matters. The lawyer is also working with Maury Rosenfelder, the receiver. We are incurring huge legal fees all the way around now. There is the wrongful death suit, the Washington lawyers for the FCC, the business sale, the receiver's costs, Ray's defense, the local law firm which appears to have over billed Ray on the station location, the employment contract Alice signed for the new station manager, etc."

"When do I get paid?"

"I'll talk to Jack."

Another month passed. Walt was sorting through his mail, began reading a letter from Jack Clafner. He went ballistic. His secretary was standing in the conference room across the hall. "How can Jack Clafner shut me off with a 'conflict of interest' statement?" he asked her, not expecting an answer.

Walt called the radio station. Herb answered as Walt yelled into the phone. "What the hell is Jack up to, Herb? How can he shut me off after all I've done? What's this about me working with Alice on the business creating a conflict with him?"

"He's the boss, Herb said. Believe me; I had nothing to do with it."

"What about the $5,000 he owes me?"

"Good luck, Walt. That's the way he does things."

"I sure as hell hope they don't need my cooperation anymore," he slammed the phone down.

Several weeks later Margaret Cole sat in front of Walt, while he explained his predicament with COLA. "Ms. Cole, I'd like to comply for Ray's divorce, but I can't produce all these records since they haven't paid me for the past year. The business statements aren't current."

"What would it take?"

"About $5,000. I believe these people have put themselves between Ray and the business. Alice told me they quit paying her rent for the office space and she has no income. They also locked her out of the building. She has payments to make on the mansion even though she doesn't live in it anymore, and the office building. Should say, her and Ray's building? They let the Indian Hills residence go back to the old owner."

"I'll talk to Ray about your money. There's enough in his retainer trust account that I can pay you if he agrees. Sorry about the mess. I do need those tax returns and other data for the property settlement."

"I can give you copies of prior work but the current work isn't completed. Actually, some of the records are in the police station from the search. I just got a call from Ray's new criminal defense attorney. He wants me to be a character witness so he can get Ray out on bail. I told them to talk to Jack, since I'm supposed to have no connection with the business any more." He looked up at the ceiling, "What a stupid situation."

Margaret was in agreement. "That's for sure. That's why I've decided to get the divorce finalized and let somebody else on my staff do the property settlement.

I won't be available for several weeks but my secretary will be in touch."

"Taking a vacation?"

"No. My sister has a medical problem. I'm donating a kidney for her."

"That's wonderful! A gift of life. You're truly a good person." He rose and gave her a big hug. Walt's opinion of attorneys improved for a short time afterward.

Alice called Detective Nelson and left her number. He returned the call an hour later. "I need to give you a new phone number and address. I won't be working at COLA any more, the station's being sold, you know." Alice gave him the new details.

"Sorry to hear that, but I guess it had to happen. We need to be able to find you for the Grand Jury testimony which will be coming up. How are you doing otherwise?"

Alice sighed with resignation. "I'm so tired of this nightmare. I carry the shotgun in the trunk of the car in case the other murderer catches up with me. I can't sleep nights. Everything is upside down. I have no money since the radio station shut me off. At least I have Bill Waters for protection."

"Bill Waters? The radio station engineer?" Nelson's mind raced through the list of suspects. "Didn't he work at the station?"

"Yes, he's staying with me and the boys at the mobile home. I'm lucky to have somebody after all this. Bye." She hung up, not wanting to go any further.

Nelson held the buzzing phone in his hand for a minute thinking, *lucky? Who's the lucky one? Maybe Bill Waters, not Alice. She's the unluckiest person I know.*

25

The Defense

Marty Tannenbaum arrived at the Ontario Red Lion on the red-eye flight the prior evening from Chicago. This morning he was dead tired even though he always traveled first class. He was dressed in his power wide-pin-striped suit which made his gut appear smaller when he stood in your face which he liked to do. In the front room there was a pot of coffee next to a large plate of fruit, melons, and various coffee rolls. The hotel suite was a spacious hospitality suite with conference table and living quarters combined. At precisely 8 A.M. his guests, Louis Cohen and David Myers arrived. They shook hands, Louis introducing his assistant. "Glad to meet you, Marty. This is Dave, my investigator."

Marty led them to the breakfast buffet. "Help yourself. It's good." As Louis walked past, Marty smelled something unpleasant on his breath. "You're not drinking this early in the morning are you?"

"Just a little Irish coffee to get started."

"Keep the Irish out of it from now on! We have work to do!"

They moved to the small conference table; yellow legal sized lined pads came out from briefcases. Marty was direct and to the point, always in control. "Here is the situation." He began by dramatically throwing the daily Woodland newspaper on the table. Opened to the local section, the headline read, 'Local Chamber of Commerce assist police doing civic duty posing as Johns to round up prostitutes on University Avenue.'

Dave sneered, "That's Victorian. Don't they have anything better to do?"

"This town is a bit behind times," Louis said.

Marty laughed, "This shit-hole of a town is in the dark ages!" They all laughed contagiously. Marty continued. "I have the crime scene testimony." He took a sheath of papers from his briefcase. Turning to Louis, he continued, "Now Louis, how long do you think it took the above mentioned cops to arrive at the murder crime scene?"

"Five minutes?"

Marty was in his face, "No, Louis. This town takes twenty minutes for violent crimes because they're busy booking hookers. That's also a 'cop-out,' excuse the term... because domestic violence kills cops. Twenty minutes is a cooling down period for chicken cops." He took a long slow sip of coffee as the message sunk in.

"It looks like that's not all." Louis said.

"Your turn, Dave. What do you think the rookie cop did when she finally arrived at the scene with Alice half-naked outside the door screaming and crying? Taped and bound, she was, too."

"I dunno. Grabbed her out of the way and cut her loose?"

"No way Jose, she pointed her little gun at the screaming, hysterical woman and asked her if she was carrying a weapon on her person."

"You're kidding, aren't you Marty?" Dave, the retired cop, responded with disbelief. "Nobody could be that stupid, even a rookie."

"Point well taken." Marty stood to make his argument so he could look down at them. "That's our case. A hick town with dumb, chickenshit cops. We need to find the holes in the evidence and win this one big. We have a rich client, a dumb town, and an unfaithful wife. All the necessary ingredients for an interesting big trial."

Louis asked, "Client Raymond turned down a plea bargain?"

"He did. I was told they offered him manslaughter with fifteen years, half-time out for good behavior. His people called us, instead."

Dave asked, "Had the bail conference yet? It'll be tough working with this guy if he is in jail all the time."

Marty sat down again after making his point. "Problem here. Our guy, Raymond, was planning to go to Argentina from Hawaii when they caught up with him. He also has no close friends to vouch for him. He didn't belong to any community service groups like the Lions Club or Rotary and didn't socialize. Even his accountant won't appear for us because he got shorted out of his bill by Ray's new avaricious business manager. Another thing to think about is that he also tried to kill a guy before, over the same wife."

Louis looked dejected. "Anything in our favor?"

Marty smiles, a cunning unscrupulous smile. He had an ace in his hat, "Everybody in the radio station wanted to kill Alice's lover for Ray. We have a strong conspiracy issue for the cuckold husband."

Louis went over to the side table, taking a bear claw. "Well, this will be fun. Agatha Christy would be proud. Maybe the jury will feel sorry for him," he said, returning.

Marty wasn't finished with his opening yet. He pointed to another article in the newspaper. "The Mayor says this place is a World Class City now with the new jail, new courthouse and planned bankruptcy court."

Louis added, "Sure, a hick town with a Third World Police Department and City Hall!"

They all laughed. Then Marty made his closing argument before they dug into the details of the discovery investigation. "We are shown as the defense by the court. Well, I want you to know that we are the offense, not the defense." He is intense. "We are going to exploit every crack, every crevice, overturn every rock, twist every angle, accuse the unaccused, and read them the Constitution until they know it backwards. That's how we are going to win this miserable case!" There were no onlookers to cheer his dissertation, but the jury would be in sooner or later and they only needed one in their favor.

26

The Second Thursday Rule

The interior of the Red Baron restaurant was decorated with old large polished wooden propellers, era matching leather flying helmets, and many other historic flying artifacts. A full-sized wooden-fabric tri-wing Fokker replica hung outside the entrance in the Woodland Municipal airport building. Small airplanes, mostly Cessna 187s and a few older smaller Pipers, buzzed past their outside patio table. Herb Rosen was apologizing to Walter Davis. "We need you. The bankruptcy receiver for the station thinks the FCC approval will be drawn out and there's a lot of financial work to be done."

"What about Jack, the enemy of the people?" Walt asked.

"I told you on the phone. He's out of it now. The whole thing is in the hands of Maury Rosenfelder the receiver, and the attorneys on the sale. You'll like working with Maury because he's a straight no-nonsense guy and takes his job seriously." He noticed the dejected look on the accountant's face. "They're serious, and will pay you promptly from now on. Jack wanted to bring in a stranger but we decided against him. Nobody knows more about the business than you."

"You know we wouldn't be talking if it weren't for Ray's divorce lawyer, paying me up."

"I know but I had no control. Jack had Ray by the balls and hung him and Alice out until Maury took over. I always felt like a mushroom around Jack. He kept me in the dark and fed me shit. The station is now running elsewhere by the LMA deal buyers. They paid us $10,000 monthly to use the license until the sale is concluded. Now they pay us interest on the 4-½ million note which is much more. I just mind the empty station and collect office rents now for Maury because they removed all the equipment." He added. "The radio station was operating on 1,000 watts back-up when we took over. The big 31,000 watt transmitter had shut down when nobody was watching the store. Ray was out of business and didn't know it!"

"My God," Walt said. "What's happening on the sale?"

Herb goes from apologetic to grim. "A little thing called the Second Thursday Ruling." A waitress, dressed like a Delta Airlines stewardess complete with scarf, suddenly appeared; they ordered a barnstormer burger plate with fries. Herb continued, "George Jackman, our extortionist, refiled another motion with the FCC to deny the license transfer and sale, claiming Ray was profiting from the sale of the business. This was part of the original laundry list of items, such as indecent broadcasting material, etc. that was filed and rejected with a letter ruling. This thing could take years."

"So what. It's his business."

"A radio station license is controlled by the FCC as a public utility. The rules are like for a liquor license. A felon or person of tainted character cannot benefit from the sale of a public utility or property."

Walt leaned over the table, "You've got to be kidding."

Herb shook his head. "I couldn't be more serious. There used to be a corporation that owned a radio station. They met every second Thursday of the month…That was what they named their business. Well, one of the owners got in trouble and the FCC told them they couldn't sell it if he profited. The corporation appealed the ruling and lost."

"Jeez. What happens now?"

"Maury Rosenfelder and the buyers refuse to give in to Jackman. They know that once they give the extortionist part of the deal he will work to get it all. Maury said he would never give in to them on his watch as custodian for the court. We have to keep Ray and the business separate. We need to sell off more real estate outside the business for legal fees. He already got a half-million from the loan on the office building… which went to the Chicago lawyers. They also got the half-million from the COLA sale."

"That's incredible. What a waste. A whole lifetime tied up and gone." He thought for a moment, with Ray out of the picture that left community property for Alice. "Are you saying you're now selling Alice's business?"

Herb nodded yes. "I need some help borrowing on forty acres of Ray's desert land in Palm Desert."

"A hard money loan?"

"Whatever you can get for him. He'll never pay it back, of course."

"Say, how was Ray able to borrow on the office building without Alice's approval." Isn't this a community property state?"

"Everything was in Ray's name. Alice was only on the residence. Everything went to the lawyers. It isn't legally right, but that's the way he did it. The lawyers also have a lien on the office building for another half a mill."

"Did you sell the record library? I'll bet Ray got a lot of money for it."

"The library…hell, what library?" Herb looked confused. "It's gone. Jack may have gotten it, along with a truckload of equipment."

"Jesus, then everything's gone. How much to the lawyers?"

"Two million so far for the criminal defense…outside the corporation. But the radio station had legal problems all over the place, too. Part of your closing the books on the corporation is the laundry list of lawyer fees owed by the business. I'll give you some data but Maury Rosenfelder will provide most of the information since the station isn't operating any more. Ray must not have anything financially or otherwise to do with the business. Maury will expect perfect statements because they will be scrutinized by the FCC and the attorneys."

Walt shook his head. "Well, I'll see what I can do on this one. This will be fun. Keeping the books on a business which isn't operating except for the benefit of the lawyers… That means the entire business statements and returns will come from non-operations. When I left off, Ray owed the business a lot of money. You will need a new lease; it has expired and needs to be renewed, and it can be bumped up to offset the corporate rents with his liability. We need to watch the corporate veil, especially with the appeals on the sale. Have the lawyers review the minute book to get the annual meetings up to date, if Ray hasn't."

"I'll talk to Maury about it. He'll probably talk or meet with you about the financials. That's not all," Herb added. "I visited Ray in jail yesterday. He's in a cell with three other inmates. Ray said William Lester Suff, the guy arrested for mass murderer, has his own cell and a television. Ray wants more privacy to work on his case. Says they go up on the roof of the jail an hour a day for exercise. He also has to lie on the floor and lift his bunk for exercise."

"Sounds tough. I heard that guys go fuzzy after a while in the tank."

"You've got it. I had to measure him for a suit, through a window."

"Doesn't he have a suit?"

"No, just an old brown thing. It wouldn't fit anyway because he's lost weight. Needs one for the trial. I paid a grand for a good suit for the trials. One other thing…"

Walt looks at him incredulously, trying to absorb the whole story.

"The whole sale… five million dollars, could disappear. Jack gets one-quarter million in commissions to broker the deal, Ray's criminal lawyers already got a million advance on the trial, we're out another million on corporate legal fees from litigating, licensing and appealing Jackman's extortion. But, the worst case…." Herb leaned over his plate, "is that Jackman could hold this thing up for years with appeals. And we could lose!" He caught his breath. "The wrongful death suit alone cost almost a million on top of the insurance settlement and the clock is still running on Jackman. You have no idea how much those Washington attorneys charge to represent us there."

Walt concluded, "Then Alice and Ray could both get zilch. Unbelievable!"

"Do me a favor," Herb was dead serious. "Don't let Alice know anything about the finances. She thinks she will be a millionaire after the sale is a done deal."

"Okay. I don't hear from her any more since she moved to the boonies with Bill Waters. Won't Ray be surprised? He used to call her and ask about her boyfriends." They finished the meal in silence, and then left together.

Several weeks later Walter called Herb from his office. He was excited. "I got the hard money loan, Herb. We got 50% of the appraisal, ten points costs, 15% interest and six months payments set aside from escrow."

"Good deal. I wonder if they realize they'll own the land?"

"Did you know what the land was for?

"Sure, the new radio station."

"Well, when Jane DeVera repossessed the new station from Ray, she found out that he owned the property for the new station and wanted to buy it."

"And Ray told her to get fucked?"

"Right on. Crazy deal all the way around. That's what the six months withheld payment was about. You know, I'll bet they never knew Ray was in jail. They never said a word when Ray's attorney signed off under the power of attorney. We told the lender he was a reclusive millionaire with gambling problems."

"By the way, Maury Rosenfelder needs the financial statements brought up to date for the FCC. They want to be sure Ray isn't getting anything out of the company."

"I know. I spoke to him yesterday on the phone. I'll watch his officer clearing accounts....that's where the station rent goes. At least that's the offset since it never gets paid. Ray still owes the corporation a lot since he took so much of it out, not on payroll. I told you to be sure he has a lease agreement, even if they have to create one. Ray's corporate lawyer will also have to get the minute book updated on these issues."

"The Receiver says the whole case hinges on Ray not benefiting from the business. That's how Jackman plans to break the deal with his appeals. Got to go now. Keep in touch, bye."

Walt was left wondering why Herb had to rush since he was tending an empty office while collecting rent from the other building tenants for the receiver; who would account for it separately for Ray and Alice. Everybody connected to the radio station seemed to be going in circles as fast as they could. Walt went back to the office to work on tax returns; it was hard to get time away during early April 1992.

Three weeks later, on April 29 the city of Los Angeles erupted with violence after the Rodney King trial in Sylmar, California. Walt drove to the radio station for a late afternoon meeting with Herb. On the way he saw palm trees near the freeway in flames.

Herb was wearing his favorite Pierre Cardin blue striped prison shirt with a prisoner number on the left sleeve. The entire discussion became the riots showing on the television Herb had on in the office. "I'd be careful about driving around with the riots and crazy people out there," he advised Walt when he left.

"No problem for an ex-paratrooper," Walt said as he opened his jacket to show the handle of a .45 automatic sticking out. "Have a permit to carry one."

Herb took a revolver out of his desk. "We don't need permits in Nevada where I come from."

The riots went away but Raymond McDade's problems didn't.

27

The Grand Jury, August 17, 1992

The old Woodland courthouse is a beautiful Grecian classic ornate structure with fluted columns in front and justice riding her winged chariot above the entrance. Alice met with Detective Nelson on the steps. "You're looking well today, Ma'am," he greeted her. Alice looked very good with her tall figure crowned by a designer casual hat. She had also taken to wearing fashion jeans which fit tightly on her well maintained form.

"Just call me Alice," she said. "I don't want my kids laughing at me like I'm starring in a western movie."

"Let's talk a minute before you go into the Grand Jury room. It's been over a year since the murder and I don't want you to be afraid of anything."

"I don't understand? What is this about?" They walked through the bronze door portals. They were inside the building with three-storied cathedral arched ceilings with bronze statues of retired prominent justices guarding their courtrooms in absentia.

Lucas Carranza walked past them carrying a bulging briefcase, really a satchel, and a huge folder of papers. He smiled and nodded to Nelson as a Deputy Sheriff opened the door to the courtroom. Nelson informed Alice about the Grand Jury process. "The Grand Jury interviews witnesses and evidence to make sure there is enough information to support the charges for the trial."

"Like a trial?"

"Sort of, except that the District Attorney presents his case and there is no Judge present. Not to worry. The testimony will be sealed until the trial."

Alice sat down on a bench in the hallway with the detective standing in front of her.

Nelson saw the fatigue on Alice's face. "Are you okay? Can you get through another hour of this ordeal?"

"The business nightmare is getting to me. The new station managers tried to get me to sign a huge personal note for legal expenses relating to the tower location and

147

I tried unsuccessfully to evict them or have them pay rent on the empty office. I still have to make the building payments from rental income." She sighed and lowered her head.

"After the murder I had nightmares. I drove with that shotgun in the trunk of my car because there are still murderers out there…that guy Snake. I was living in the prison of a house with a man I don't love and the love of my life is gone. My life is over." She lowered her head and began softly crying. She looked up, tears irrigating her makeup. "I still have nightmares, but not of the crime. The nightmare is that Ray will be let free and I'll be back where I started."

"Keep your head up, Alice. We can't change the past but have to go ahead."

"For what? You know Ray did it."

"That's why there are Grand Juries and trials. Just keep your head up and tell what you know."

"Strange things keep happening. Like the storage place incident."

"What storage place?" Nelson asked, wondering if he missed some evidence.

"Last week I was unloading boxes from a green car into a storage unit with a garage door, the kind that you pull up… I suddenly realized that I had a dream about this several years before the murder. I dreamed I was unloading boxes from a green car into a garage," she paused. "But I didn't own a green car when I had the dream."

"Someday it'll all be over. Professor Lucas will take care of Raymond."

"Professor Lucas?"

"Yes, he's the prosecutor. The man who just went in. Not really a college professor but he is very thorough and always gets his man."

"This whole thing is crazy. You know Ray treated this whole thing like a business transaction. Just write a check to get Tom murdered or write another check to get your wife back."

The courtroom door opened; a moment later the Deputy motioned for Detective Nelson to enter. "They'll call you," he told her and went into the courtroom.

Inside the hot courtroom the Grand Jury Foreman called the jury to order and commenced to roll call the other eighteen jurors. Three District Attorney lawyers, the court transcriber, and Detective Nelson were also present. Lucas Carranza addressed the jurors. "I would like to explain the indictment process: The charges we expect to prove today are based on the evidence, and witnesses we will hear." He paused, surveying the nervous group to assure that he had their attention and that everybody had a grand jury handbook. He continued, "Count one is Penal Code Section 187, murder; in this case, first-degree murder. Count two is conspiracy to commit murder. Underneath that count are overt acts 1,2,3,4, and 5. Count three is violation of 459 of the Penal Code; that is first-degree burglary. Count four is false imprisonment and the victim is Alice McDade. Count five, the solicitation for murder." He continued describing the particulars of each count. Then he detailed the investigation, walking in front of the jurors to get their individual attention and confidence.

He then admonished the jurors. "Before we bring in the witnesses, remember that we need a strong suspicion standard to apply to every factual and legal determination. Unlike a trial jury, you do not have to find an unreasonable doubt. Any questions?"

"It's hot in here." A juror wiped his forehead with a handkerchief.

"They're working on it. One side is working."

"Sure, the other side," the juror added.

After answering questions from the jurors about the guidelines in the handbook, Lucas called the first witness, Alice.

Lucas Carranza and Detective Nelson hung behind in the jury room at the end of the day after the jurors had all gone home. The other lawyers had been interviewed earlier and dismissed, so they could get back to work, after testifying about their participation in the plea-bargain confession of Domingo Malichera, and the mansion and radio station search. "Well, partner, one more day and then we're on the way." Lucas said.

"Do you think they'll approve all the counts?" Nelson asked.

"You should know better than to ask me. That's like asking me if I did my homework." They laughed lightly together and left.

The next day the Grand Jury convened to continue reviewing the witnesses and evidence. At the end of the day the foreman handed a document to Lucas. The indictments showed 'guilty' checked off on all counts listed.

Marty Tannenbaum and Louis Cohen were ushered into a small room in the old jail where they met with Raymond McDade. The room appeared to be a temporary structure, with moveable walls like hotel conference rooms. It was carved out of a larger room along with two others, symptomatic of the overcrowded jail. The Deputy gave the lawyers a contemptuous look, slowly closing the door. Marty walked over to the door and could hear the Deputy breathing on the other side. "Goddamn it!" he told Ray and Louis. "There's no privacy here!" Then he moved Ray to the opposite side of the table so that he would be speaking toward the door with his soft voice and the louder lawyers the other way.

Marty noticed Ray's fatigue and apprehension. "Our conversation is privileged. Tell me whatever I need to know. It won't get any further than this room. Just do as I say and you'll be a free man."

Ray nodded, "I didn't do it, you know. What happened on my jail bond hearing? I need to get out of here to work with the case. They have me in a cell with two other guys."

"We tried. I even flew down from Chicago to get to a judge and they wouldn't give me a hearing. They claim that you tried to leave the country and have denied bail consideration." Marty opened his briefcase, took out a dozen notebooks. "Fucking jailers! They scrambled my notes when they searched my briefcase." Then he found the one he wanted. "Now, Ray, on the night of the murder you rented a car."

"Yes. I don't remember why."

"You have a dozen cars. Could it be they are all antiques and you had to leave a good one off at a garage overnight for repairs?"

"Sure, that was it," Ray said. "An air conditioner problem."

Marty gave him a lined pad and pencil to write with. "Now write down the name of the garage you think you left it with." Ray began writing. "Where did you hear about Argentina not extraditing Americans?" Marty asked.

"Maybe I read it someplace."

"Could Detective Nelson have mentioned it to Alice and she told you?"

Ray looked up. "Now that I think of it…that could be."

"Good. Now write it down."

The session went on for two hours when the Deputy suddenly entered the room. "Time's up, fellows," he announced. Ray got up. The Deputy snatched the pencil from him and gave it to Marty. "Too dangerous to have pencils longer than two inches," he said.

When the deputy left, Louis said, "Don't quote me, but that Deputy has a two-inch dick."

All the lawyers were in the courtroom of Judge Sandy Lewis at the September 18, 1992 hearing in the huge new court building that was like an office building full of courtrooms. Lucas Carranza, Marty Tannenbaum and Louis Cohen rose as the elderly Judge entered. The judge used a cane to get to his seat, and then banged it loudly across the top of his desk to gain their attention. Raymond sat uncomfortably in the jury box wearing a prison-orange jumpsuit, his waist and legs chained to black and Hispanic males. *I'm part of a chain gang,* he thought dismally, as they would be attached until each prisoner had been called before the Judge.

Louis Cohen began his argument in his strongest most forceful voice. "Your Honor, we would like to consider a Post Indictment Subpoena."

"Denied."

"Your Honor. We would like an unsealed copy of the Grand Jury transcripts."

"You have ten days to ask for them. Denied, because of unfair pre trial publicity. You can make a motion about unfair trial publicity. I'll deny it, anyway." The judge had no patience with the out-of-town big lawyers, especially when in pain from his gout.

Louis responded, "I'll ask ten days notice to file."

"Separate issue. Will set date."

A clerk handed a copy of the indictments to Louis. "I need four weeks minimum to prepare this extremely complex case."

"Denied. Try Judge Matthew Clarke. My calendar is too busy. Set trial readiness conference in 3-4 weeks."

"My client's visiting rights have been restricted, Sixth Amendment, Rights of Counsel. Want to resubmit motion about guards being present, other issues."

"Is this a motion?"

"Yes, a motion to dismiss based on bad prisoner treatment by the jailers. Resubmitted."

"We take exception to the declaration against the Sheriff's Department," Lucas said.

"No orders at this time. Set it with Judge Clarke next week." The judge looked at them for further business. Seeing none, he began reading the next report in front of him without excusing Marty.

Raymond watched in dismay as the attorneys collected their briefcases. He was chain-ganged to the others for their cases to be heard. The court ordeal was beginning. Something inside wanted to scream, but couldn't. He found it hard to rationalize that he was really in this surreal place. After all, he didn't murder Tom; Domingo Malichera did it...

The lawyers left, Marty encountering an oversized deputy at the door who shoved Louis aside as he attempted to punch him in the face. They broke off, cursing each other. That was how the War of the Lawyer's began.

28
Prelude To Trial, 1993

There was a quiet period before the trial, similar to the deadening silence when birds know a raptor is in their midst. At first the imminent trial was on the horizon; then it disappeared for more than a year.

The Chicago lawyers filed numerous motions to throw out testimony and statements, expunge evidence, purge testimony, disqualify witnesses, raise Constitutional issues, and disqualify the entire case. The smoke screen went on with weekly motions sometimes from Chicago and sometimes prepared overnight, as if on a whim, by the corresponding California lawyers. After a year of legal wrangling, it then became almost impossible to find agreeable non-conflicting trial dates between both sides for the prolonged conflict.

One morning, Nelson, leaving a trial, met with Lucas in the new courthouse. They stopped for coffee outside. "Did you know there was a conspiracy between Bill Waters and Alice McDade?" Lucas said. "Justifiable homicide was the latest motion for dismissal from the esteemed Chicagoans."

"No surprise. Especially since they're married now. After Alice's love of her life was murdered, she marries a hired hand for protection. Just like Patty Hearst and her bodyguard. What about Ray's prior conviction? He has a pattern of premeditated violence. If he gets off, we should see that he gets turned loose in Chicago."

"Only after he finishes off Bill Waters."

"Nelson, did you hear about the taped conversation between you and the DA's office when you searched the McDade mansion?

"No. What happened?"

"Ray had a hidden tape recorder under his bed; so he could keep track of his wandering wife. Well, he taped the phone call about taking the computer evidence during the search. Now, Louis is saying he had justifiable cause to flee."

"Interesting fellow, Ray. Hear anything about the divorce attorney's letter that we took during the search?

"They're saying it was confidential between an attorney and his client so it must be tossed. It's an interesting piece of evidence because it outlined how little he was going to let Alice have for her marital property. You missed the mini-trial this past month on Ray's mental competence and memory loss. There was a great parade of highly paid professionals testifying to his inability to stand trial."

"I heard it was dismissed for lack of evidence."

"Took six days of testimony, though. This thing has become my career. I think I will put Raymond McDade Trial Specialist on my resume."

"I told you, Lucas. This work is much more interesting than the usual plea bargain."

"The scary part is that we can do a perfect job and lose the case to the jury. I'd sure hate to go through all of this to see the murderer go free."

Detective Nelson dutifully filled in the gaps of the investigation caused by Ray's disappearance. He communicated with the Department of State for information on Ray's phony passport. He visited Maui, met with the postal clerk and Richard Hussack. There was the drive to San Diego to follow the resurrection trail of Ronald Alwin. Nelson visited Ray's landlady, the D.M.V., the cemetery to find poor Ronald's grave marker, the site of Ray's car wash employment and found an employment application at a San Diego hospital. Nelson silently acknowledged Ray's brilliant scheme to become Ronald Alwin and how he almost got to Argentina. *I find it hard to believe,* he thought as he drove back to Woodland from San Diego, *that anybody thrown into this situation could put it together unless they were a spy in the CIA.* There was Nelson's trip to Washington to visit the salesman Alice had stayed with, and local visits to the home of Mary and Paul Sloan, now residing near the military airbase in San Bernardino. The Department of State gladly sent their case records of Ray's phony passport investigation by mail.

Alice was also an infrequent visitor to Nelson's office to help him complete his gaps in the crime testimony. Once Alice asked him why Domingo would murder teen-agers over a few dollars. "I know you won't believe me, Alice. Domingo didn't kill them for money. I believe that when he killed Tom, he found that he liked killing people. It gave him power he never had before. He's a sociopath, that is, he has no feelings of remorse or compassion for his victims." She put her hand over her mouth and gasped in astonishment at this knowledge of a person she had worked with for several years. Nelson was saddened after she left; understanding her secret better than most, her weakness in life was as a victim of an endless search for love.

The accountant Walter Davis, Herb Rosen managing the empty station, and the COLA bankruptcy receiver, Maury Rosenfelder, kept in touch over the financial statements, gossip about the trial, and the endless extortion litigation holding the COLA sale up at the FCC. The only cash flow to the hollow business entity was quarterly interest paid on the big sale note which would be paid off when the FCC litigation succeeded. Nobody would talk about what would happen if they lost to the extortionists. Walter called Herb after months of silence.

"Herb, thanks for the check for Ray's tax returns."

"You were lucky to get it," Herb said. "We established a petty cash fund from station office equipment sales. This pays Rays prison incidentals without involving the COLA Corporation."

"What are you doing to keep busy these days?" Walt said.

"I'm down to two days a week now. I was retired before so now I'm returning from light retirement to deep retirement."

"Do you still see Alice?"

"Yeah, she's living in a mobile home out in the sticks. Has a local clerical position and lives with the big guy Bill Waters, who she married. Pops and the kids live with her, too. They are barely getting by because we can only pay her a stipend for now."

"What's the ex-station operator doing now?"

"He's the babysitter. He takes care of Pops and the two boys."

"I wonder what the property settlement looks like." Walt said.

"No property settlement yet. She still thinks she's going to get millions from the sale. By the way, did you know that there was a lawsuit filed for Manuel Rodriguez, the teenage boy who survived the shooting?"

"Yes, yesterday I was handed a subpoena by a beautiful young dark haired girl, the daughter and process server of the suing attorneys. At least I'll get a day in court with you since I'll be paid to testify for the corporate operations," Walt said.

"Too bad about Ray's insurance company settling the first trial for much more than the coverage, leaving the business on the hook for the balance." Herb said

"I know, Herb. Everybody is sue happy except for the victims of Tom Winters' death, his children, father, and ex-wife. I heard they needed financial aid because the children required extensive therapy and treatment. Why haven't they sued, too?"

"They're afraid of the exposure. Just can't cope emotionally with the trial and all."

Maury Rosenfelder suffered from cancer but clung to his goal to outlive the endless extortion appeals by front man George Jackman and his backers. He adhered religiously to the fiduciary commitment of his assignment by the court which forbids forfeiting any COLA's assets to outsiders. Perhaps it helped that he was not a member of the Bar, yet his wife was an attorney. Unpaid COLA legal bills mounted into the millions. Then there was another knife in his side from the extortionists. He called Walt. "Walt, I'm getting a hard time on the inter company transactions between Ray and the business. We need to restate the statements for the past two years to show the rent account separate."

"That's a lot of work, Maury. There's nothing wrong with combining the accounts. It doesn't make sense to have a rent payable account payable to Ray and a separate officer's loan account from Ray without offsetting the balances."

"Sorry, Walt, but that's what the guys in Washington are demanding. They said the accounts have to be kept separate and need the statements redone right away."

"Hell, Maury. That's a ton of typing."

"But we have to do it, because they are saying it could blow the sale up by merging funds."

"Where are we on the sale?" Walt said.

"We won the last FCC suit but it was appealed and the above item was brought up for the Second Thursday Rule. The extortionists are hoping to get the property sale voided and reallocated to them as a political allocation."

"I'll get back on the statements when I have time."

"Damn it, Walt. I need them redone now and don't have funds to pay you to do it."

The COLA buyers marked time. They earned huge amounts from combining parallel advertising programming of both Country Western and Rock and Roll. The first thing they did was to change the COLA format to Oldies. Disc jockeys were now in the background with their endless commercials. The initial $10,000 LMA fee payments and later interest on the sale note was only a small fraction of the combined earning power. The lucrative deal continued with many nervous people who would one day pay off the remaining $4.5 million owed to conclude the sale, or lose the station and half-million deposit altogether.

Money and women, Detective Nelson had once told Alice, were the reason for most murders. He should have added power, which is the sum of the two for a complete equation.

29

The Trial Begins, June 1, 1994

Criminal attorneys dread the weekend before a trial. Only their spouses and children hated it more because most big trials begin on a Monday, the lost weekend dedicated to the preparation and organization for the crucial period.

On the Saturday before the Raymond McDade trial, the phone rang at Lucas Carranza's office. "Lucas, I thought I would call to give you my support…moral and mental that is, for the big event," Detective Nelson said.

"Much appreciated, buddy. I think we will need all the help we can get. Maybe a prayer, as well. These guys seem to have an unlimited budget for papering the system with bullshit. I have never seen so much stuff since I've been in the business."

"Yeah, this guy Raymond's guilty as sin but he has all the money in the world to get off. Boss, I know we have a great case but I think it will be a contest. I hate that guy Marty, who's always quoting the Constitution as if he were on the Supreme Court. He has a lot of people in the back room doing his homework for him too."

"That's for the jury, not us. In fact, while pandering to the jury they try to rewrite the constitution."

"Lucas, I've always wondered…I know you could make a lot of money on the other side, and I wondered why you never crossed the line to work for the bad guys."

"Don't think I haven't thought about it. I know I could make five or ten times as much money working for guys like Ray, and they would probably stand in line to get me, but I didn't go to law school to make money. I went there to practice the law. I know there is a lot of injustice in the world but I feel good doing my part to correct it. Besides, I detest the guys who take all that money to try and fool the jury to get their criminals off. I really do."

"Well, that's a great answer. See you in court…On demand that is, Partner."

"Nelson, many thanks for getting me all the discovery evidence I needed. I owe you and Carlson a lot. Bye." He hung up. Yes, Lucas thought, *I could be rich, but*

I like to sleep nights. And I don't like the thought of helping the bad guys get loose on the streets.

The trial began in the new courthouse. Discussion immediately began on pretrial points and authorities between Judge Matthew Clarke, Lucas Carranza, Louis Cohen, and Marty Tannenbaum. The Judge began, "About the prior Paul Sloan indictment, which shows intent, I don't want a trial within a trial on this issue."

Marty wouldn't let it go. "That was 16 years ago. You know McDade has a substantial lack of memory."

"Not at all. Now, about the jury, I need good estimates for the time on this case."

"About four weeks."

"About four to six weeks." Marty added.

The Judge continued, "I have a 21 question thing for the jurors. We need to time-hardship qualify them first. We can six-pack them in, you each have 20 preemptory challenges. I don't want any surprises about new witnesses or longer sessions." He looked directly at Marty. "I won't let you unring the bell on jurors."

Lucas brought up an issue, "The defendant should wear his toupee because the witnesses saw it on him."

Louis formalized. "I ask the Court to consider whether he will be required to wear that in front of the jury."

"I'll reserve that right," the Judge answered.

"I'll have the property room people look for it. It looks like an old bird's nest," Lucas said.

Marty said, "It would be unfair to plunk that thing on his head. Wearing a toupee requires some preparation, so he doesn't look foolish. I understand the reason they're not worn in jail because other inmates pooh-pooh them and ruin or wreck them."

"Let me cut you short there. If I order it worn, I'll make sure it's not just stuck on his head. No in-view-of –jury-placement. What does it require?" the Judge asked.

"I don't know," Marty replied, "because I don't have one. Well, he wants to wear it. I know it's needed for witness ID." Marty thought, *this trial is going to be a real piece of cake with every miniscule item a debatable issue. His client would get his moneys worth.*

On the ninth of June, the surviving jurors and alternates were ushered to their seats. Lucas Carranza in his best dark suit...the one never worn to work at the office, Raymond McDade in a loose-fitting stunning blue suit with a white shirt and red tie, Judge Matthew Clarke on the bench, Marty Tannenbaum, and Louis Cohen were all present at their tables. Lucas began the opening statement to the jurors.

"Thank you for the lengthy jury selection process. Things should proceed faster now." He breathed deeply, "Mr. and Mrs. McDade had a marital relationship which soured after 20 years in late 1990. Mrs. McDade sought consolation, warmth in another relationship, the victim, Tom Winters. The relationship became romantic and she left her husband after Christmas." He paused, "Mr. McDade told her repeatedly that if Mr. Winters were out of the picture they would be back together." Lucas walked to his table to look at his notes and give the jury a minute to digest. "Mr. McDade then offered $5,000 to the victim to leave her... He refused. Then he offered the same $5,000 to Domingo Malichera, an unstable young man. But Mr. Malichera didn't own a gun so the defendant gave him two $500 checks to buy one and he did." The jurors were now intently leaning over the counter, listening to every word. "Mr. Malichera entered the victim's apartment on February 19, 1991, found Mrs. McDade there, tied her up and shot the victim when he came home." Lucas stopped walking in front of the jurors. "The obsession resulting in the victim's death had been lifelong, taking another form of violence in 1978 when Mrs. McDade first left her husband." Lucas took a deep breath. "On January 26, 1978. Mr. McDade went to the residence of lifetime friends demanding they tell where Mrs. McDade was, and accused Paul Sloan of having an affair. Then he attempted to shoot him. I'll provide the evidence and details later. Mrs. McDade was in another state with another man at the time." Pause. "You will see a number of witnesses testify and many details. I believe there will only be one just and true verdict: that he is guilty on all counts. Thank you."

He turned to the Judge, said, "Thank you, Your Honor." And went to his table.

"Thank you, Counsel." The Judge acknowledged, and then addressed Marty Tannenbaum. "You may make your opening statement."

Marty placed his stout figure in front of the jury, looking sternly at each of them at eye level. "My name is Marty Tannenbaum. I am a lawyer and I represent, with two attorneys, the defendant Mr. McDade. I will examine and cross-examine witnesses in this court and act as Mr. McDade's advocate, his attorney. You know what the prosecutor's job is, to present evidence to you. And your job in this system is to take that oath of office seriously. There will be contradictions in testimony; there will be exact opposite testimony on various points. It's eventually going to be up to you to determine the credibility of witnesses and His Honor will instruct you as to the indicia...what to look for and whether or not you think they're telling the truth or not." He opened a pad of notes, continuing. "What Lucas Carranza told you today, the prosecutor, is not evidence. Just an attempt to get you started. It's your determination as to whether or not the evidence rises to that very high level."

Lucas Carranza stood up, "Excuse me, Your Honor..."

Marty continued, "...To beyond a reasonable doubt."

Judge Clarke interrupted: "Counsel...I don't object to some preliminary opening remarks as to how the jury is to perform their function but I would like to keep the content of your argument to what you intend to prove in this case."

Marty continued unperturbed. "What you will hear, ladies and gentlemen, is a very strange, weird, sometimes confusing, contradictory state of affairs...the 'exploitation' of Raymond McDade." Marty walked silently past the jury box from one end to the other for his point to sink in. "This shy and retiring brilliant gentleman had considerable business success by saving his money and working many, many hours in a very successful radio station business." Marty went to his table for a glass of water. "You will hear that he loved Alice McDade and loves her to this day… that time spent in his radio station was an effort to provide the safe secure environment for his little family… that his life's work was to provide a nice home and income for his little family… Now keep in mind that Raymond McDade was not charged with any criminal offense arising out of what happened in 1978. Keep in mind that Alice McDade went astray, became 'unfaithful' to him, consistently deceived her husband while on secret rendezvous with Tom Winters, her lover." Marty held his hands up in despair. "You will hear that they exchanged marriage vows again, at his suggestion, and that he put the radio station up for sale to save their marriage. Then she left him again but also left her extended family, her own mother, two children, and father-in-law in the house Raymond built for them." He paused for a half-minute. "After abandoning her family she was returning to the secret place of living with Tom Winters and found herself looking down a rifle barrel."

"You'll hear her say she wasn't frightened. She was never hurt and Tom Winters was murdered, died instantaneously by the stone cold-blooded murderer who made a deal… with the prosecutor for life in prison without possibility of parole." Marty raised his voice, "Now that sounds like pretty heavy-duty punishment, doesn't it? But you will hear that he not only killed Tom Winters but that he had killed a thirteen-year old boy in another cold blooded execution and tried to kill and indeed shot another fourteen-year old boy in Badlands. He knew at the time he made the deal with the prosecutor that, indeed, he was making a deal with the Devil for the killings!" Marty stepped back for the expected objection.

"Objection. Argumentative," Lucas said.

"Sustained."

"You will hear that he recognized that for these murderous deeds, he would be executed by the state under the death penalty law. He will also say he deserved it and to avoid that penalty for these heinous crimes, he made a deal. A deal to testify 'falsely' about Mr. McDade, that Mr. McDade put him up to the murder of Tom Winters. When you hear Domingo testify… His Honor will instruct you about the degree of trust you should give his testimony."

"Excuse me, Your Honor." Lucas protested. "I object to that. He's not supposed to be instructing the jury."

"Sustained."

"Now, indeed, you will hear that Alice McDade, shortly after the murder, married Bill Waters, the employee at the radio station to whom Raymond McDade had confided. You will also hear that during a search of Mr. McDade's home he heard a conversation between two Deputy Attorneys that his perception of the conversation was so inappropriate and improper that he felt he was about to be framed and wrongfully accused of a crime that he did not commit and got scared, panicked, and fled. Raymond McDade has the mantle, the cloak, of being an innocent man." Marty posed for the jury, smiled to his wigless client, and received a dark contemptuous stare from Lucas.

That evening Lucas skipped dinner. While the children and his wife, Mary were watching the news on television he sat in his den reciting the terms Marty used in the trial: the exploitation, unfaithful wife, deal with the Devil, instantaneous death, false testimony, inappropriate and improper framing and wrongly accused, and most of all…the mantle and cloak of an innocent man.

Mary entered, saw his dilemma and put her arm around him. "You know," he told her, "I feel like I'm the one on trial. That is, the law is on trial."

"Look at me, Lucas. These people may be evil and unscrupulous but you always whip them." She smiled at him. "Come to the kitchen and get something to eat."

Lucas followed her to the kitchen. On the way, she looked back over her shoulder, "Remember the big case….the Patty Hearst case…that made those lawyers famous?"

"Sure. They invented the brainwashing defense to show she wasn't responsible for her own actions because she was kidnapped."

"Well, she went to jail didn't she?"

"Sure, got a Presidential pardon by Carter to get off later on."

Mary turned and with her simple 'I told you' smile concluding, "Doesn't that mean they lost the case then? They got famous for having a famous client, not for winning the case."

Lucas smiled, because he knew he could always win at home no matter how tough the case.

30

Alice's Testimony

Alice McDade was wearing a tight-fitting salmon-colored designer suit when Lucas Carranza began the examination. "Mrs. Waters, were you formally married to the defendant, Raymond McDade?"

"Yes, I was."

"Are you presently divorced?"

"From him, yes."

"And you are married to Bill Waters?"

"Yes."

"Did you play a role in the business?"

"Yes, I worked side by side with him for a long time. Very long hours."

"Was it 24 hours a day?"

"Well, it seemed like 24 hours a day with beepers, always something."

"Would you describe him as a workaholic? Did it strain the marriage?"

"Yes."

"When did you start to see Mr. Winters?"

"I met him at work in September, 1990. He was my nursing instructor."

"Did you get romantically involved?"

"Yes. In December, 1990."

"Did you ever tell the defendant about your relationship with Mr. Winters?"

"Yes, because there were times when Ray was making sexual advances I didn't want anymore. I couldn't…I just wanted to be with Tom."

"Did you go to counseling?"

Yes. It didn't work. He would say, 'If Tom would just go away, things would be fine. You'd be home. You'd come back to us."

"Did he blame Tom for your problems?"

"Yes, always."

"Did you ever confront your husband about an offer he made to Tom?"

"Oh, God!" Alice lost control, 'I told him, 'You can't buy people'! I told Ray, 'you can't be calling him and offering…offering him money to back away from me. You can't do that. That's not going to bring me back'."

"Did you tell him the amount?"

"Yes," Alice stared at Ray across the courtroom. "Five thousand dollars."

Judge Clarke intervened, "Excuse me. Would you like to take a moment?"

"No! I want this over!"

Lucas continued, "Did your husband admit or deny it?"

"No. He told me he didn't care. Just wanted me back."

"Did you and Mr. Winters stop seeing each other?"

"No. Tom loved me." Alice brought out a handkerchief and dabbed her eyes.

"For the record," Lucas faced the Court. "I'm opening this sealed manila envelope marked exhibit #24…for identification." The envelope is stuck together from the silver duct tape contents. "I'm not going to be able to get this out without ripping the bag to shreds. Let me open it up and peel it back a little bit. I hope all the jurors can see this." He held it up for them to view, then faced Alice. "Is this the tape used on you during the murder?"

"Yes."

"The record should reflect I'm opening sealed evidence envelope #23 for identification." He turned to Alice. "Do you recognize this?"

"Uh-huh."

"What am I holding up? Appears to be a black stocking cap."

"The cap they put over my head."

The next morning the lawyers were called before the bench. The jury was held back. Marty opened, "Your Honor, I'd like to call to the Court's attention the fact that the Court had a colloquy with me and Mr. Carranza in which you said, 'I have complete confidence in Counsel'. Then Mr. Carranza, in a voice which could be heard by all the jurors, said, 'I'm glad somebody does!' Jurors should not hear that kind of conduct!"

"Mr. Carranza?" the Judge asked, remembering the scene which he must expose for public record.

Lucas was pissed. "I wasn't facing them. Probably the frustration that we are going so slow. It's appearing that Counsel is being intentionally dilatory in looking through the exhibits. First the defendant has to see it, then the Counsel, then the jury, then the witnesses, and on and on. The jury took five minutes to see the composite drawing on a sheet of paper they had already seen. They have a copy of it in their notes. We are weeks into the trial and getting worn down."

Marty continued as if Lucas had not spoken, "Just briefly. I heard the words and, in my opinion, they were loud enough for the jury to hear. I would also…"

The Judge stopped him. "Did the reporter get it?" He looked to the reporter, "Reporter, did you hear?"

"No, Your honor."

The Judge answered impatiently to the lawyers, "My response is that I don't want any more outbursts in front of the jury. I'm getting frustrated with the case. We know who the actual murderer was and that it actually occurred in the apartment. Yet we're spending all this time looking at things. And quite frankly, we shouldn't waste twenty minutes each day reviewing exhibits more than once. Unless I'm missing something, unless we're saying that Mrs. Waters is somehow an accomplice or set up the killing, then we are wasting time here."

Marty stirred the issue, "That might be, Your Honor, depending on the evidence that's advanced here."

Judge Clark looked hard at Marty. "Deputy, call in the jurors."

Alice was back on the witness stand. Marty asked. "You described your husband as a workaholic, Mrs. McDade?

"Waters, please."

"I'm sorry, Mrs. Waters. During the time you worked side by side, you were an alcoholic too... workaholic too; is that correct?"

"Yes." "You corrected me when I called you Mrs. McDade. Tell us when you married Mr. Waters?"

"October 31, 1992."

"Now, you described your relationship with Mary Sloan. Been friends since grade school? Correct?"

Since the age of eight."

"That relationship, closeness as sisters, does it continue until today?"

"Yes."

"And, nevertheless, you had sexual intercourse with her husband, is that correct?"

"Yes." Alice held her chin up.

Marty looked at the jury. "And you didn't tell her, did you?"

"No."

"And you didn't tell your husband about that, did you?"

"No."

"Now, you testified that you had marital problems with your husband in 1978. Were there legal documents of separation?" Marty held his notes up.

"No. I never told him I was leaving."

"You just left?"

"And you left with another man, not Mr. Sloan?"

"Yes, for two months."

Marty raised his voice, "And during that time you had sexual intercourse with him, too?"

Lucas interjected, "Objection. Irrelevant!"

"Sustained."

"May I be heard, Your Honor."

"No." Clarke said. *This is a trial, not a circus,* he reminded himself.

Marty turned to Alice. "Did you tell your husband or family where you went?"

'No.'

"Whose name did you use in Washington?"

"I—Irrelevant"—Lucas objected. Judge Clarke answered, in very strong terms: "Sustained. Have the reporter outside. I'll listen to counsel."

The lawyers and Judge adjourned to a conference room nearby. "There is a pattern of deception which amounts to a breach of credibility, Marty said. In fact some of the pattern of credibility amounts to perjurious conduct in which she lied under oath."

"The only problem I'm having is following you," the Judge said. "Certainly we've heard on direct all of her adulterous relationships. I guess my next question is where does that stop? Is she on trial or is Mr. McDade? In other words, she wasn't the victim of this crime. Certainly Mr. McDade had a motive to do what he did because here's a woman that's out there having adulterous relationships with everyone she can come in contact with. So now the defense wants to show this and that she lies…"

"Indeed, this witness, herself had a motive to see Mr. Winters dead." Marty adduced.

Lucas countered, "Your Honor, if there is evidence of third-party culpability, especially Mrs. McDade then I think we need an offer of proof from counsel. Motive is not enough. I also have an objection of going through the past twenty years of her life…whether she didn't drop money in the poor box, or whatever. We're really confusing things here. Let's get to the important times."

Marty again. "I have offers of proof from discovery already for the Court to examine…."

Judge Clarke was getting angry, "I already ruled there wasn't any third-party culpability coming in. I reviewed your points and authorities before. Why do you think she's an accomplice?"

"Statements made in her presence, which she concealed… wherein indicated they intended to kill Mr. Winters. Bill Waters, her new husband, offered to 'mess him up and rub him out' to Mr. McDade…. Then he moved in with Alice McDade after her husband was incarcerated."

Lucas countered Marty, "I brought this whole issue up on a motion because I didn't want to be standing in the hallway when this came up, which is exactly what is happening."

"Right," confirmed the Judge.

Lucas added, "The motion that this Court heard and ruled on is the same exact subject the Counsel is now offering to reintroduce in violation of the Court's order. How is Mrs. Waters an accomplice? I'll tell you right now, for the record, I'm not calling Mr. Waters to the stand. I need proof, first."

"I don't want to go through another, 'Didn't you have sex,'" Judge Clarke said. My ruling right now is that if you call Mr. Waters I want that done outside the presence of the jury!"

"Judge, I do have another motion in writing and was going to request the Court allow a voir dire of Mr. Waters."

"You would have to," Judge Clarke added.

Lucas spoke, "I have a concern that jurors will speculate, you know, 'She married this guy' and without evidence about it. I have a concern about this incorrect third-party culpability, getting it in the back door when you can't get it in the front door."

Judge Clarke banged his gavel. "I'm not going to allow any inquiry at this point. Let's break for lunch now."

They convened for lunch. Lucas called home, "Wha's happenin'" he asked, thinking of their favorite Cheech Marin movie.

"Not much, wetback. How's the trial going?" Mary asked.

"Marty's trying to say Alice is an accomplice. Make her dirty, planned to knock her boyfriend off."

"Can he do that?" Mary asked.

"He's trying. At least he's trying to instill doubt in the jury and that could cause a mistrial or 'not guilty' if he succeeds."

"Honey, just do your best. I have faith in you."

"Well," he laughed, "Don't forget the prayer."

That afternoon Alice McDade-Waters was back on the witness stand. Marty began the questioning. "Mrs. Waters, after you left the marital home, moved in with Mr. Winters, you abandoned your children and mother?"

Lucas objected, "Objection. Argumentative, compound."

"Sustained."

"When you went to live with Mr. Winters, you didn't live with your children, did you?"

"No."

"You didn't live with your mother, did you?"

The examination went on and on for the remainder of the day and the next.

The following evening Lucas went to the china cabinet, took out an unopened gift quart of Jack Daniels, poured a glass.

Mary was suddenly behind him. "But Lucas, you don't drink," she said.

He sipped the bourbon. "Until this trial is over I'll need a boost now and then to relax and sleep. The defense are trying to make Alice out to be unfaithful... justifying Ray's homicide."

"Oh, God." Mary took the glass and sipped. "Aren't we all? I was thinking religiously...all sex seems to be forbidden to Catholic girls from parochial schools."

31

The Coroner, The Fourth Of July

Lucas had the Woodland County Coroner on the witness stand. He knew he had to refute the opening remark and lie from Marty about Tom Winters dying instantly.

"Mr. Koi, are you a medical doctor?"

"Yes, I graduated medical school in Kwangju, Korea and completed my internship in the United States."

"What particular field?"

"In the pathology. Later as a forensic pathologist."

"So you're a medical doctor that examines people who have been killed?"

"Yes, and I look for the causes of death."

"Where do you work as a pathologist?"

"Woodland Coroner's office from 1971."

"Did you have occasion to do an autopsy on February 22nd 1991, on an individual named Tom Winters?"

"Yes."

"Did you find anything significant on Mr. Winter's body?"

"A headshot wound on the left side of the head."

Lucas produced a photograph marked exhibit #38. "Do you observe the bullet wound you described?"

"Yes."

"Did you notice any tattooing or gunpowder residue around that wound?"

"No. The wound appears to be a distant gunshot wound, since there is no soot or powder or tattooing. At least two feet away."

"Did you find anything significant in his head area?"

"Yes. A bullet which caused the head injury. The bullet perforated through the skull on the left side as far as the right side. It passed through his brain and stopped under the skin on the right side of the head."

"Were you able to determine the path the bullet took?"

"Yes, with a probe."

"Was the bullet the cause of death?"

"Yes, from aspiration. The...during the autopsy I examined the airway and it showed blood seeped through the fracture, the skull, and soaked into the lungs. The aspiration meant inhaling the blood." There was a sigh from somebody in the jury box.

"And then releasing the blood through the mouth or nostrils?" Lucas said.

"Your Honor, I have an objection to the line of continuing questioning, it's a waste of time." Marty said.

"Excuse me, Your Honor, I object to the comment." Lucas said.

"Yes, that comment will be stricken."

The coroner was given more photographs. "Do you see the blood on the wall and the drapes?" Lucas asked.

"Yes, from the aspiration."

"Does that also indicate that aspiration of blood, that the victim survived for some minutes?"

"Yes."

"Then, in your professional opinion would you say the victim died instantly?"

"No. He died minutes later... drowning as his lungs filled up with blood."

Lucas gave a long look at Marty who deliberately looked away, then let the witness go.

The trial dragged on for the whole month. On June 30, 1994 a pretrial conference was held in the chambers. "We have a long weekend coming up," Judge Clarke told them. "Let's schedule our witnesses so they don't have to come back in the middle of testimony."

"By the way Your Honor," Marty piped up. "I'm not going back to Chicago over the long weekend. Do you know of a barbecue I could attend?"

The Judge smiled coyly. *No Chicago politicians here,* he thought. "No. I only attend other people's barbeques."

Marty stared blankly back at the Judge and Lucas.

Later that morning they brought Raymond McDade into the courtroom. There were no jurors present. Ray had huge circles under bloodshot sleepless eyes. He wore no toupee.

Judge Clarke addressed the three attorneys and the defendant. "We have this letter from Mr. McDade's attorney marked personal and confidential, which was recovered during the search of his residence."

"I submit that it is material to the trial because it discusses the divorce settlement," Lucas volunteered.

The Judge disagreed. "But it is marked confidential and falls within the attorney/client privilege."

"It's not hide-the-ball, Judge. The letter mentions Alice changing her mind on the divorce settlement," Marty said. "It's after she was living with Tom Winters and his lawyer says, 'after meeting with your wife and you I have reservations about resolving this matter amicably.' This is material to our case because it involves the rejection of the car and residence offer which results in the business sale."

"I'm not going to let him go into the contents of the letter," Judge Clarke said.

Marty tried again, "I'm not suggesting you de-publish it to the jury by striking out information on cross-examination."

Clarke said, "My ruling is going to be that we're not going to use the letter and envelope. You can ask your client whether he met with his wife at the lawyer's office and what happened."

During the noon break, Lucas visited the Police Department next door for lunch with Detective Nelson. They went to Art's Grille nearby where they found a seat in the crowded bar and ordered a sandwich. "How's it going," he asked Nelson over the lunch crowd noise. "Still gathering pieces for the William Lester Suff murders?"

"Yeah."

"Busy guy, wasn't he."

"We have evidence on a dozen prostitute murders, mostly very poor young girls from University Avenue. The problem is that we really don't know how many more there are out there." Nelson was nursing a cup of coffee; Lucas, a diet soft drink.

"At least a psychopath should be easier to convict than a murderer with the erudite Chicago lawyers. The deciding issue will be when Raymond McDade testifies this afternoon."

"Why so?"

"I simply don't know what to expect from his conniving defense lawyers. They simply twist everything around and I have to keep proving them wrong. It's like the prosecution is on trial, not them."

"Well, hang in there, Lucas. After all, it's only been a month now," Nelson joked.

"And a million dollars of wasted taxpayer money," Lucas groused. "You missed the big one this morning, Coroner Koi's testimony. He works in the ivy covered mausoleum behind the new court house."

"You mean the place with the notice on the door to take deliveries to the rear?"

"You've got the right place. How many bodies do you think he has carved up in his illustrious career?"

"Maybe a thousand, Lucas? Am I close?"

"How about 20,000 not counting the ones he only supervised."

"You saved that one for lunchtime, didn't you?"

"Sure, I want to be sure our detectives can take it. Enjoying the hamburger?" He slapped Nelson on the back, and grimly headed over to the courthouse. *McDade didn't have to testify,* he thought as he went through the metal detector, that means *that he will be sprinkling gunpowder over Marty's flames, unless they have testimony Lucas didn't know about.* What Lucas didn't know was how well the rehearsal between Marty and Ray would play out.

32

Raymond Mcdade Testifies

The morning began with Raymond McDade, thin and nervous because his life depended on his testimony, on the witness stand. The jury was present in a courtroom packed with reporters, onlookers, friends, and the curious. Marty Tannenbaum began the examination. "Mr. McDade, how many hours a week did you work when you first took COLA over?"

"Fifty or sixty hours a week."

"And how many hours a week were you working on your job for the other radio station at the same time?"

"At least forty hours a week."

"You heard your ex-wife describe you as a workaholic. Was it true, Sir?"

"Yes, I just wanted to provide for my family, kids. That's all."

"Would you tell us what happened on Christmas Day, 1977?"

"I found a note in the kitchen from my wife saying she was leaving. It just said vaguely, 'Dear Ray, I'm leaving you.'"

"And had she already left?"

"Yes, the closets were empty."

"Did she say where she was going?"

"No. She told nobody. Just disappeared."

Marty held up his hands, looked down. Marty continued. "Did you visit Paul Sloan looking for your missing wife?"

"Yes. A neighbor said she was having an affair with him."

"A shot was fired at that meeting?"

Ray was apologetic, looked at the jury. "I thought the safety was on. I was just trying to scare him to find out where she was."

"Were you arrested?"

"Yes, I was found guilty of a misdemeanor, brandishing a weapon."

173

"Was Alice having sexual intercourse with Paul Sloan?"

"Yes, he testifies so here in court."

"Did she return home?"

"Yes, after three months. She told me she lived with another man in Washington."

Lucas objected, "Hearsay."

"Sustained."

"Move to strike the answer," Lucas added.

Judge Clark struck it.

"Did your wife leave you again?"

"Yes, after Christmas, 1990."

"Did she tell you where she was going?"

"She said she was still seeing Tom but was going to live with a girlfriend from work."

"Who was Bill Waters?"

"He was a supervisor at the radio station."

"Did you confide in him concerning your marital difficulties?"

"Yes, and Domingo found out because they worked together."

"Did he suggest that he could go down and rough Tom Winters up?"

"Yes, I told him I was strictly against it and definitely... you know, 'whatever you do, do not harm this person.'" With a long sad face, Ray looked over to the jury for them to see that he was truly an old, tired innocent man being framed. He didn't see what he wanted.

"He had a roommate, a Colonel somebody?"

"Yes, a mercenary who got Soldier of Fortune magazines. Bill said the guy could make Tom disappear. 'I said 'no way.' This is, you know, insane.'"

"Did Bill have other statements?"

"He offered to find a prostitute or girl to go to bed with Tom and have Alice catch them or take pictures of it. That's..."

Marty looked at the jury. "That's fine. That's fine."

The court recessed for lunch. Marty met with his assistant attorney at the Courthouse Bar & Grille. They waited in the buffet serving line. "How are we doing?" Marty asked.

"We have the jury by the balls," Cohen said. "Did you see their look when Ray testified about the note the bitch left him?" he mimicked Alice, "'I'm leaving you Ray, Bye, Bye'"

"Sure did. We can discuss that at dinner tonight instead of working late at the hotel. Maybe over a little Irish Whiskey."

After lunch outside the courtroom Prosecutor Carranza bumped into Detective Nelson. Lucas flashed a pair of World Cup tickets at him. "Lucky guy." Nelson said.

"I'm going with my father for Father's Day. Hope the trial doesn't interfere because I hope to get off early Friday."

"Stay lucky!" Nelson told him as they went their ways.

Raymond was back in the witness box. Marty asked, "Did you loan Mr. Malichera money?"

"Yes, $500 to get his car fixed." He looked past Marty at the jury. "Wait a minute, I also advanced him another $500 when he said it cost more the next day."

"What happened when you lived in the Indian Hills residence?"

"Alice came home, said there was a warrant out for my arrest. I wanted to… you know…call my attorney. Turn myself in, get it over with."

"What happened then?

"Alice said to leave, hide, even though I felt I had no reason to. She said to visit business friends in Hawaii."

"Did you want to leave?"

"No. I was scared of flying and afraid I'd get arrested for something I didn't do. Alice drove me to the airport, anyway."

"Why did you go back to Los Angeles?"

"To clear my name."

"Did you ever pay Domingo Malichera $5,000 for anything?"

"No. Just his salary."

"Did you ever conspire with him or anyone else to kill Tom Winters?"

"No. Never. I never did anything like that."

"Do you understand that you're under oath in this court today?"

"Yes, Sir. I'm telling the truth."

Judge Clarke dismissed the court for the noon break

Lucas saw Detective Nelson at the door. They moved to a conference room to escape the gaggle of jurors in the hallways.

"I never saw such a lying man, Marty and Raymond," Lucas said. "Now I know why Marty didn't want the Deputy around when he met with Ray. They were rehearsing the show. Its surreal hearing him lie so much." Lucas said.

Nelson chuckled. "Don't they teach you that in law school?"

"Not the school I went to. I suppose that when a man's future is on the line, like with Ray, he would probably kill again if it would get him off. What's happening to bring you here?"

"Got some good news for a change. We know who the other murderer, Snake is. He's a friend of Malicheras', name's Jose. A guy called, and said Snake-Jose boasted about the hit."

"Do we have him in custody?"

"Not yet. Wanted to talk to you first."

"Don't pick him up until this trial is over. I don't want those bastards hanging things up on us. We are already past five weeks. He wouldn't help the case anyway since Malichera worked directly with Ray."

"Okay, boss. Alice will be happy when we put this guy away. She thinks he's still looking for her. Where do you think the trial is going?"

"Well, I picked the jurors for this one. Let's see if I can show them the difference between the truth and fiction."

"This little man is nobody's hero."

Lucas returned for the cross-examination of Raymond McDade. He had a mandate to turn the case around at this point forward or it could be lost. "Mr. McDade, you wanted to clear your name when you heard there was an arrest warrant?"

"Yes, Sir. It was important."

"And you called Detective Nelson to discuss with him the things you discussed today? You did that?"

"I tried to get him with no avail."

"And you said this was an important thing, clearing your name. And you went down to the Woodland Police Department because you couldn't get a hold of him that one time?"

"No. Counsel advised against it."

"You also used false identification in order to clear your name while you were hiding from the police?"

"No. I was keeping a low profile. I wasn't hiding."

"Was this part of a plan to avoid arrest?"

"Yes."

"And part of the plan was to find Ronald Alwin's name on a gravestone and you think, 'Hey, that's a good one,' right?"

"Yes."

"And you went to the library and took other steps to get a false birth certificate?"

"Yes. Alice and Waters suggested it."

"Alice and Bill Waters walked through the graveyard with you?"

"No. I did that."

"You took that information to the Social Security office for a form? And you lied to the clerk about who you were, didn't you? You didn't tell them, 'I'm Raymond McDade, and I want to get a Social Security card in somebody else's name,' did you?"

"I just filled out a form."

"And you went down there to the Department of Motor Vehicles? And you lied to the clerk even signing an oath on the form, that you were Ronald Alwin didn't you?"

"Yes, I don't recall the oath."

"Remember the Postal clerk when you filled out the passport application? Do you remember that he swears people in to make sure they're telling the true information?"

"Yes, but I don't recall swearing in."

"Do you recall there is an oath under the signature line on the form?"

"You moved from San Diego because your landlord gave you notice to leave?"

"That's true."

"You ended up in Indian hills? And you were introduced to the landlord as Alice's brother, right?"

"Alice introduced me as her brother."

"You were standing right there?"

"Yes."

"Did you correct her? 'Hey, wait a minute. I'm not your brother, I'm your husband.' Did you correct her?"

"No." Raymond bit his lip.

"You didn't want to be at your mansion where the police had been?"

"No…yes."

"You called Detective Nelson and said, 'I'm down here in Indian Hills using this false name. Come and talk to me about the case?"

"I didn't do that."

"Then you went to hide in Maui, right. And said, 'Hey, can I come over and live there for a while because I'm having marital problems'-- right?"

"Yes, I stayed with a friend there."

"And you told him, 'Look, you know, I'm tied up in this murder. I didn't do anything. I'm innocent. I want to clear my name.' You told him about the murder, Alice's boyfriend, search warrants? Did you tell him any of that, Mr. McDade?"

"Yes, I did."

"You enlisted Richard Hussack to help you hide from the police?"

"No. I just asked for advice."

"You had business cards with Ronald Alwin printed on them and deceived people every time you handed out one?"

"I only handed out one card."

"You deceived that person. You didn't say, 'Wait a minute. I'm Raymond McDade. This isn't really my name. I'm wanted in Woodland for murder?'"

"No."

The Judge called a recess, noting that several jurors appeared to need a bathroom break. He admonished the jury not to discuss the case outside the courtroom. Twenty minutes later they were herded back into the courtroom. Lucas resumed.

 "Mr. McDade you were on your way to Argentina after coming back to Los Angeles to clear your name?"

"No, I didn't have a passport."

"But you had travel brochures and a ticket for Argentina dated ten days after the Los Angeles trip?

"I had thought about it."

"You found out Argentina didn't have an extradition treaty with the U.S.?"

"That's what Alice told me that Detective Nelson told her."

"Now, let me see if I understand this. The detective who's trying to arrest you is giving your wife information about where you can hide?"

"That's correct." Ray wiped perspiration off his lip.

"You wanted to leave the country to be safe from the police? So you wouldn't have a trial like we're having today, right?"

"I would hope there would be an ongoing investigation."

"Did you ever talk to Domingo Malichera about your marital problems or Tom Winters?"

"No. He was just an engineer."

"He was basically a nobody." Lucas said. "I mean, he just made minimum wage, not close to him as friends?"

"True. He possibly approached me or asked me."

"You told Detective Nelson you and Domingo Malichera had a conversation about killing Tom Winters, Mr. McDade?"

"He…Domingo said something…about…something to the effect, um, he needed another notch in his gun."

"About killing Tom Winters, right?"

"I don't recall. Bill Waters was present. Malichera mentioned it. I didn't say anything."

"So he told you he wanted to kill Tom Winters. He's just walking by, and he says, 'Oh, by the way, I want to kill Tom Winters.'"

"No. I was walking by."

"So you were walking by, and he stopped and said, 'I want to kill Tom. I want another notch in my belt'?"

"Well, Bill Waters wanted to rough him up and Malichera said, 'I need another notch in my gun."

"Bill Waters said he wanted to rough him up and then Domingo said, 'let me shoot him for you?'"

"Something to that effect. And I…chuckled. Then Bill laughed…and you know…."

"So you were talking about killing Tom Waters?"

"Yes, that is, they were talking about it."

"You didn't say a word? They were talking about your marital problems and killing Tom Winters?"

"I don't recall the conversation."

"You aren't trying to deceive the jury, are you? Lucas looked at the jurors, seeing some shaking their heads or staring away. "You wouldn't even think of doing that, would you?"

"Exactly."

Another recess was called.

The jury filed out. Lucas found Nelson in the audience.

"After this testimony, I expect Jesus to be on the stand for the defense," Nelson said.

"I'm glad you didn't go to Argentina with Ray because I need you here." Lucas added. They laughed and went past the security checkers to soak a few minutes of sun on the stairs outside.

Later he was examining Ray again. "You have told the court that you were a workaholic but the persistent problem about your marriage was the time you weren't spending at home?"

"Well, she, you know, was making demands like the Hillcrest mansion. I didn't want to buy it; she did."

"She was money-hungry; with you just because of your money? Because you were rich? She didn't love you for yourself?"

"Well, she did a credit check on me when we first dated. She never needed anything afterward."

"Didn't you tell her that if she testified against you, you would let the sizeable asset, the radio station go and she would get nothing? That the divorce settlement was still pending?

"That is…what's the question?"

"Didn't you tell Alice that you would let the property go if she testified against you? Didn't you tell her that on the phone while you were in jail, Mr. McDade?"

"I don't recall that."

"Don't you have a house worth a million dollars and a multi-million dollar office building to be divided on divorce settlement?"

"We had a simple agreement where she would get a car, house and monthly check. She didn't want the business."

"You didn't get an agreement on it?"

"We'd gotten back together."

"Well, your divorce lawyer never told you there was going to be a problem with the property settlement?"

"He said, 'No problem.'"

"But there was a problem after you did get divorced. There was a change of heart by Alice about splitting those valuable assets which were community property?"

"Later, after she married Bill Waters."

"But didn't you receive a letter before that from your lawyer saying Alice had a problem with the settlement?"

"I don't recall a letter. He just said she would have to get her own attorney."

The Judge called a recess for a lawyer conference. Marty said, "The letter from Ray's attorney was protected by client-attorney confidentiality. The letter was marked 'personal and confidential.'"

The Judge answered, "There's a problem with the defendant talking about a marital agreement and then invoking a privilege when he's saying contra to the agreement."

"Your Honor, it was taken from him through the search warrant," Marty said. "It shouldn't have been taken."

"He doesn't have carte blanche to commit perjury," Lucas said. "We could call Mrs. Waters to testify about the letter."

Marty leaned forward. "I would like to strike the questioning and answers concerning this subject."

"No." The Judge said.

"I'm not suggesting you de-publish it to the jury." Marty said.

"No." The Judge shook his head. "I wouldn't because, quite frankly, I think I can let it in with an abundance of caution."

Then the Judge dismissed the jury for the day.

The next morning Lucas faced Ray again. He hoped he was tiring less than Raymond who had bad County prison food working against him. "After Christmas when Alice moved out to be with another man, were you thinking about, 'Hey, she is going to divorce me,' right?"

Ray stared at Lucas. "It crossed my mind."

"And you tried to persuade her to come back to you and to stay in the marital relationship, right?"

"Yes."

"And all during this time you're not thinking about community property interests in your millions of assets? And the impending divorce represented a threat to those assets, right?"

"I had never… didn't think about it."

"Before Mr. Winters was killed you were aware she was a threat to the radio station which must have been pretty important to you?"

"I just loved the work. I wanted to leave the station to my sons."

"You advertised the station for sale to satisfy Alice and you would leave the business to keep her?"

"Yes, for thirty million dollars."

"And you knew before Mr. Winters was killed that she would get half of the thirty million if she divorced you, you knew that, right?"

"I hadn't thought about it."

"You also talked to her about having another child, didn't you? And you pleaded with her, 'Let's have another child. Leave Tom and let's stay together.'"

"Yes."

"You threatened to commit suicide?"

"It wasn't a threat, was a question."

"Not a threat? 'Shouldn't I just commit suicide so you can have everything?'"

"I never said that."

Lucas had an endless list of questions on his yellow pad. *Always ask the question you have the answer for,* he thought. He also saw how clever his witness was. "You called Tom Winters before he was killed?"

"Yes, just to talk with him."

"You didn't call to persuade him to leave your wife alone, did you?"

"No. I was bringing it to his attention that she was married."

"By telling him, 'Hey, your girlfriend is married,' to help him out and do him a favor?"

"No, I liked him."

"He was dating your wife and you liked him, even though you had reasons not to like him?"

"I couldn't dislike a man I never met."

"Didn't he know you were married from the voice message on the telephone when he called about the party?"

"I'm not sure."

"But after Mr. Winters was murdered, didn't you show your station engineer a newspaper clipping and Mr. Castleberry said, 'Jeez, that's terrible,' and you said, 'That guy stole my wife?'"

"Never."

"Did you ever visit the residence of the murder victim?"

"I may have…to look for furniture missing from my house."

"With a key you made."

"No."

"Did you ever call the victim at work and threaten to kill him?"

"No. I'm not a violent person."

Lucas added, "Except in 1978 when you visited Paul Sloan with a gun in your pocket?"

"It was in the glove compartment."

"And you had extra bullets in your pocket?"

"I don't remember."

"You were there because you had been told he was sleeping with your wife."

"That is correct. But I just wanted to find out where Alice was. I was concerned and didn't want to embarrass him in front of his wife."

"You pointed it at him, telling him to get in the car, as he testified."

"Oh, that's a lie. Never happened." Ray squirmed in the seat, but his voice level held constant as Marty said, so the jury would believe him.

"You were just showing him the gun? You didn't threaten to kill him?"

"That's true."

"You didn't shoot at him as he ran back to the house?"

"It fired by accident. I almost shot my foot off. It was frightening."

"The police arrived and you were arrested, weren't you?"

"That's true."

"And you were surprised when the arresting officer told you Paul pressed charges and you said, "'Can you imagine that? Some friends.'"

"I assume I may have said that."

"And so that's what you learned; that you shouldn't do that directly."

"Well, okay."

"So the next time the situation came up again in 1991, didn't it? Wife left you for somebody else?"

"Yes."

"And you had more to lose. The station had become more valuable."

"I hadn't thought about that, but I…"

Lucas pressed on. "So the stakes were bigger, weren't they? You had more to lose?"

"I hadn't thought about it." Ray repeated his cop-out answer.

"You told Alice you could make the marriage work if Winters was out of the picture?"

"I don't recall. No."

"Why did you rent a car the day of the murder?"

"I had to leave the car off at the garage. Air conditioner problem."

"How many cars did you own at that time?"

"Fourteen. But they were all vintage cars being restored except the other old van which had a bad power steering leak."

"And you needed help to go from the garage to the rental agency. So, the only person you could find to help you was the fruitcake Malichera while he was on time off from work?"

"Back then I don't recall any opinion of him. That was three years ago."

"You told Detective Nelson he was a fruitcake. Didn't you?"

"I—if that's what it says."

The witness was excused. A recess was called by the Judge. Even a jury of blind men could see Ray lied all the time. Raymond earned a gold star for his coordinated wife-destroying testimony with Marty. Domingo Malichera's testimony next week would complete the case one way or the other.

33

Domingo Malichera Testifies

The prosecution team celebrated the Fourth of July at Lucas's place. Teenage children screamed in the pool, the women gossiped. It was a collective joy when they gathered. Lucas, Nelson, the other two attorneys, and Carlson gathered before the television with beers in hand. Their minds were elsewhere and the small talk about the ballgame turned to business. "What witnesses do we have left?" Carlson asked, knowing he was on the list.

"You, for one, our best evidence guy, with your murderous bullet." Lucas answered. The other men grinned or smiled. "Then there was the criminologist from the Sacramento crime lab, who tested the gun. We also have the State Department on the passport fraud and the auto mechanic who never saw Raymond or his car."

"And Malichera, the fruitcake murderer." Nelson added.

"I expect a plea bargain argument from the enemy on that one." Lucas replied. "He already brought it out in his opening speech, 'the pact with the Devil'."

The men laughed out so loud the women stopped talking and looked in from the living room.

One of the novice lawyers asked the inevitable question. "Lucas, do you think we have won the case?"

Lucas thought a minute, "There is always a problem even when we have a case, where you guys did fantastic work gathering evidence and we have a good presentation. And we couldn't ask for a better Judge than Clarke because he is level enough to take the enemy crap without blowing his cool and endangering the case for appeal. Yet, these bad guys question, distort, and twist every single event. They're doing everything they can to confuse the jury. We are really on the defensive undoing everything that Marty and Ray say and do. Now, I believe we have done a perfect job of gathering and presenting our evidence because everybody in the universe knows this guy Raymond, had the poor soul murdered, but the jury is questionable. We can have all the pieces lined up and a single juror, instead of going along with the others, could balk or be obstinate or deliberately stupid or liberal enough to believe the enemy. Then we get a hung jury and we're back where we started with a retrial or letting the bastard off. It's not a case of Henry Fonda turning the jury around on a decision; it's a case of a rogue individual that makes the collective decision bad."

"You know," Carlson said. "You're so good in court that we should buy you one of the powdered white wigs the English barristers wear. Then you could wear it when you're practicing in front of the mirror." He held his beer can up and they all toasted Lucas.

"Don't get excited yet, guys. The trial isn't over until it's over. I expect the enemy to open up with a whole new list of lies to throw the jury off in his closing arguments. I could end up wearing Raymond's rug instead of the powdered white one. Besides, on my salary I couldn't afford the powder for the wig."

"It's crazy," one of the novice attorneys said. "That the enemy law firm gets almost two million dollars to get Raymond off."

"Correction, to conspire jointly and severally with him," Nelson said. "And we get regular little paychecks to prove the bad guy Raymond is guilty, even though everybody knows he's guilty as sin."

"Justice is fair, but the pay isn't," Carlson added. "That's why so few cases get to trial. A fair argument for the cost saving and face saving miracle of plea bargaining," the novice attorney said.

"The County is spending a million to put Raymond away, then millions more in that expensive prison afterward to keep him alive," Nelson added. "I guess it's all about money. If I don't make my house payment, they take it away."

"The bad guys always have bigger houses," Carlson said.

Later that afternoon Nelson cornered Lucas at the garage refrigerator where the case of beer had been stored. They were all a bit inebriated and loose by then. "Boss, you look kinda worn out this summer. Are you thinking of moving on, joining the guys on the other side for the big money?"

"I'm lucky that I have the greatest evidence detectives in the world and that the District Attorney leaves me alone and I have a good judge on this case. That's why we have such a high kill ratio of cases. But I'm awful tired of this business now. I just don't want to do it for another five or ten years."

"You didn't answer my question, Boss."

"Well," Lucas said, "I'm thinking of going into politics. I think it's the next level for me and I can really do some good there."

"You have my vote, and the vote of everybody who knows you." Nelson said, as he reached out to grab Lucas' hand, but since he had a beer in it, placed a condensing hand on his bosses shoulder instead.

"At any rate," he paused, "we have a week to go with the trial and I want you guys to know how proud I am that you gave me everything I needed. The rest is up to the jury." Tears mysteriously appeared in his eyes and he excused himself for the bathroom. *Shouldn't get so emotional about these things,* he thought. *Got to get out of the business, am getting too involved.*

The week began with a conference concerning Malichera's testimony. Louis Cohen said, "In the Allen case the Court indicates that if an accomplice or witness is placed under a strong compulsion to testify in a particular fashion, the testimony is tainted beyond redemption and denies the defendant a fair trial. We feel the District Attorney has set themselves up as the definer of the truth for Mr. Malichera."

"I believe the Court has the plea bargain file. Mr. Carranza?" The Judge asked.

"I reviewed the memorandum of agreement but the Allen case argued that their plea bargain was based on mistrial testimony which is not relevant here."

Louis countered, "Mr. Malichera had a strong compulsion to testify in conformity because he had to escape the death penalty."

"I'll look at the agreement again," the Judge said, "but don't believe he was conditioned to lie to change his sentence."

Lucas changed the subject, "I request that Mr. Malichera be placed in the witness box so he doesn't have to rattle all the way up there."

"Well, I don't know why he shouldn't be rattled with his chains like any other witness or receive special treatment," Marty commented.

"Mr. Carranza?" the Judge asked.

"…And he is going to be in his jail-issue uniform?"

"We didn't put chains on any other witnesses, either," The Judge added.

"That's correct," Marty commented, "He is what he is."

The Judge ruled, "We'll bring him out just the way he is."

They called in the jury and Domingo Malichera rattled, handcuffed to waist and leg irons to the stand. He looked defiantly into space or the courtroom ceiling. Lucas faced him. "Mr. Malichera, you currently live in the Woodland County jail?"

"Yeah."

"Where did you work?"

"COLA radio station, for Raymond McDade." He pointed to Ray. Ray tried not to smile back, held his hand up a little bit.

"How much did you earn?"

"A little over six dollars."

"How did you learn about Mr. McDade's marital problems?"

"Alice called one night looking for him. She talked to me. Then Ray told me he had problems at home."

"What did he say about his problem?"

"Well, he told me…gave him a lot of headaches. And…he wanted to somehow cure him."

"How did he want to cure it?"

"He wanted to know if he could hire somebody to kill him. I said I can get somebody."

"Okay. Did he ever ask you to do it?"

"Yeah. He said he would give me $5,000.

"Did he give you money up front?"

"Yeah. In two different checks for the gun."

Photocopies of the checks were shown him for identification. "Do you recognize these checks?"

"Yeah, they're for the gun."

"Are they paychecks?"

"No. These were to get rid of Winters."

"Did you use that money to buy a .38 caliber handgun?"

"Yes, I did. From somebody on the street."

"Were you to receive any other money after you killed Tom Winters?"

"Yeah, half before and half after. He had to, he owed it."

"Did he tell you what Mr. Winters looked like?"

"Yeah. He told me he rode a Harley Davidson motorcycle, wore leathers. Had a beard and glasses."

"Did you go to the apartment according to the first plan?"

"Yeah. At night. I waited two or three hours in the parking lot, but he didn't come out."

"Did you talk to Mr. McDade afterward?"

"Yeah. I told him it was a dumb plan. Ray had a new plan. Going into the apartment. He gave me a key and rented a car."

"Let me jump back in time for a second. Did Mr. McDade ever tell you he had talked to Mr. Winters?"

Malichera was tiring, having trouble getting his thoughts together. "Well, yeah. He told me, um; one time…he was going to give him some money to…lay back his wife."

"What do you mean by 'lay back his wife'?" A street language answer.

"Oh, stop seeing her. He offered a lot of money."

"Do you remember the figure?"

"No."

"So you were at the apartment. Who came in?"

"Alice. We tied her up, covered her face. Put her in the bedroom." He smiled weirdly, "She was terrified, scared."

"Then what?" The jury was alert now, all leaning toward Malichera as wheat before the wind.

"There was a buzzer and he called to warn Alice he was coming."

"And when he came through the door, what happened?"

"We set him down on the couch and I walked up, and I blew him away." Suddenly there were people stirring and squirming in the jury box and people speaking in the audience.

"Where did you shoot him?"

"In the left temple."

There was a gasp in the courtroom.

"With the gun I showed you earlier?"

"Yeah. Then we took off."

"When did you give Mr. McDade the car keys back?"

"When I went to work the next day. I told him Tom was dead. 'I want my money'."

"Was the $4,000 in cash?"

"Yeah, in an envelope."

Mr. Malichera, a couple of months later you got arrested. Is that right?"

"Yeah."

"And you went to court and pled guilty. Is that right?"

"And do you remember signing a form with your lawyer?" *This was the crucial item, the plea bargain,* Lucas thought. *The case could rest on this.*

"Yeah." The plea bargain agreement was produced. He recognized it.

"Do you remember what the agreement was?"

"Yeah. Life in prison."

"Life without parole?"

"Yeah."

The court recessed the jury for lunch. On the way out, voir dire examination was made of Domingo Malichera before the Judge and the attorneys.

Louis Cohen asked, "Mr. Malichera, did you work for a gentleman by the name of Bill Waters?"

"Yeah. Did I work with him some?"

"Yeah," Louis responded, "Do you remember him?"

"Yeah, he's the big fat guy who trained me."

They broke for lunch. Domingo went out the back, chains dragging behind, and the jurors filed out the front.

That afternoon the jurors were led from the assembly area to their places.

It was Marty's turn, "How old are you, Sir?"

"Twenty-three." Dom Malichera answered.

"Did you go to high school?"

Lucas objected, "irrelevant".

"Sustained."

Marty protested, "May it please the Court?" he asked the Judge.

"It's still sustained."

"May I be heard on it?"

"No." the Judge snapped back. Marty's endless meaningless objections and conferences to gain a minute edge on the trial had worn him down during the drawn-out sixth week of trial.

Marty resumed, "Did the Badlands detective ever ask you, 'Did Ray ever talk to you about killing some dude'?"

"Yeah. Ray talked."

"Speak up, please. You're not afraid of anything here today, are you?"

"Not at you."

"Not at me. Anybody else?"

"I ain't afraid of nobody!"

"You weren't afraid when you pulled the trigger and killed Tom Winters, were you?"

"So what, Man?"

"Right. 'So what?' And you weren't afraid when you killed a fourteen-year-old boy up in Badlands, were you?"

"That was a long time ago."

"Can you hear me?"

"Hey, I didn't know he was fourteen!"

"You didn't know he was fourteen. How old did you think he was?"

"Objection, irrelevant," Lucas said.

"Sustained."

"Do you remember you shot another young boy up there, too?"

"Yeah."

"What did you do when you got to the apartment where you murdered Mr. Winters?"

"We went in, used the keys, put the stuff in bags."

"What stuff?"

"Stereo equipment."

"You ripped the place off, right?" Marty moved too close to Malichera who didn't like people in his face.

"Well, yeah, big dummy!" He yelled back.

"What did you say?" Marty yelled.

"You heard me."

"No. I didn't hear you. I'm sorry."

"I said you're a dummy." Malichera looked back at Marty.

"I'm a dummy!" Marty walked by the jurors so they could see what a dummy lawyer looked like. "Do you remember, when you went to the Grand Jury, that you raised your right hand and swore to tell the truth, the whole truth, and nothing but the truth, so help you God?" Marty was shifting to the Constitution again, Marty, the keeper of the law.

"Yeah."

"And what happens if you don't tell the truth?"

"I don't know. You tell me." Malichera snapped back. His patience, what little of it that was left, was worn out...

"Do you remember lying when the Badlands detective asked you if you killed Tom Winters?" Marty tried to trick him into a wrong answer.

"I said I killed him."

"When you spoke to the detective did you tell him your associate was named Snake? Later called him David?"

"I don't remember that. That's somebody else's name, anyways."

"Who? Someone else you know? You were lying to him, weren't you?"

"I got mixed up, dummy!"

"But you did give him the name, Snake. Right? And the name David, and Jose?"

"Hey, I was in a lot of pressure then."

"So you lied to…"

"You better back off man!" Dom's chains restrained him from punching the heavy lawyer. He had a hair-trigger temper.

"So you lied?"

"Hey, you better calm down."

"Mr. Tannenbaum, step back please!" The Judge said.

 "When you blew Mr. Winters away, how far was the gun from his head?"

"Not too far."

"How far?"

"I don't know, Man."

"Show me your hands. How far?"

"You tell me Man, you got the report."

Marty gave up and moved on, "You were told you would not be executed if you agreed to testify against Raymond McDade, correct?"

"That was the agreement."

"Do you know that if you lie, the agreement is null and void at the option of the District Attorney?"

"I don't recall. My lawyer was there."

"You understood it in order to keep from being put to death. Correct?"

"Yeah."

Lucas sighed as the judge shut the court down. Tomorrow was closing arguments and Marty's lies would have to be countered again. Marty could give Raymond his keys to freedom. The big day was finally here after years of preparation. Another sleepless night lay ahead.

34

Closing Arguments, Friday July 8, 1994

It was the lawyer's final day. Initial closing argument to the jurors began with Lucas. He was tired, as was Marty, having spent the evening before preparing handwritten summations.

He took a deep breath and began. "The defendant had two obsessions in his life, his radio station and his ex-wife. These obsessions caused him to plan and complete a murder, the act of murder, the killing of another human being, someone who would not be able to talk and experience things ever again with his family or friends. His life is over because of the defendant's obsessions. You might feel sympathy for him about his unfaithful wife. But we're here to determine the facts." He moved back to his corner table, took a sip of water, slowly returned and continued.

"The radio station was the most important thing to him and he had thirty million reasons to kill this man because it was threatened. The other obsession was his wife. He taped phone calls, tried to hire investigators, followed her around. He tried to murder Paul Sloan when he thought he had sexual relations with his wife. The same situation presented itself in 1991 and he reacted similarly to rid himself of the person seeing his wife." He slowed down because the jurors were taking notes.

"You heard so many ridiculous stories from the defendant. He was deceptive, lied to people, filed false documents to deceive you. Is everybody lying other than the defendant or is the defendant the liar? He is a very clever man with a learning curve, who discovered that the second time his wife left him; he could hire somebody to murder the person, instead of doing it himself. His wife found somebody who loved her and left him. Mr. McDade then planned to get him out of the picture." Lucas returned to his table where he fidgeted with his notes a moment to let the jury absorb and record his remarks on their legal pads.

"Dom Malichera is a nobody, making minimum wage working the graveyard shift. Ray hires him providing all the materials to do the murder. Dom is caught after another murder and confesses, providing information about Mr. McDade's involvement. The plea bargain was on August 21, 1991, months after he confessed the crime. Who do you hire for the murder? Not the village priest but an unstable guy working for minimum wage." The jury was tiring, looking confused as they took their notes, sometimes looking sideways at the other jurors. Lucas paused.

"Killing a person unlawfully, as in this case, is first degree murder. It is also premeditated with willful intent. Mr. McDade also committed special circumstances for a financial gain… the $5,000 payment, and the defendant aided and abetted it. The other charges, conspiracy, was the agreement between Dom Malichera and Mr. McDade. It had overt acts of giving Dom Malichera checks, keys, and a rental car. The burglary count is satisfied by taking Tom Winter's property from a residence." He paused because the jurors were all writing furiously. "You will weigh the evidence and follow the written instructions which His Honor will talk about. Justice is blind. It doesn't matter if the defendant is somebody like Dom Malichera or a millionaire."

A recess was called for lunch. After they returned, it was Marty's turn. He was wearing a totally black suit with faint pinstripes. He looked like a mortician in his power outfit. His technique was to overpower the jury with his powerful attitude and constitutional rhetoric. He began with his deepest voice. "Ladies and gentlemen of the jury, there are some things which are not in dispute. I submit that Dom Malichera is a stone-cold cold-blooded murderer. We can agree that Alice McDade abandoned her husband on Christmas Day sixteen years ago without warning. We can agree that he loved her very much and went to the Sloans because he believed she was having an affair. Then he displayed a gun. Brandished it, as you heard. The Police report doesn't mention any bullet hole in the door." He paced back and forth before the jury.

"Don't be distracted or led astray with over 100 bits of information. That's why I am discussing them now. There's no dispute that Dom Malichera murdered Mr. Winters, that he was, 'blown away,' in Dom Malichera's words. He expressed no emotion, even had a hamburger dinner after a cold-blooded murder several hours earlier." Marty drifted back to the table for more notes and a glass of water.

"You heard the tape with the district attorneys casting lots to try the case, laughing and joking. He fled because he was being unjustly accused and convicted of a crime he did not commit. All based on child killer Malichera's word. He panicked and changed his identity. Don't waste your time with it in the jury room. Not important. The District Attorney urges you to diffuse and obfuscate the truth." He paused. "Now, Mr. McDade comes home from San Diego to find Mr. Bill Waters living there with his forever untrustworthy demon of a wife. We can also agree that Alice was always the boss, in control, came home saying, 'I want you out of here because there's a warrant for your arrest.' This is the same woman who said, 'If I thought he had anything to do with the murder, I would have killed Ray, myself.' Innocent men flee when accused and scared." Marty walked the jury path again smiling at a pretty young lady. *I wish you were in Chicago,* he thought.

"What is in dispute here is that the prosecutor utterly failed to prove that Raymond McDade had an agreement with Dom Malichera to kill Tom Winters. Can you believe Dom Malichera, after observing his character in the courtroom? 'I don't know, dummy, you're the dummy.'" Marty laughed out loud for effect. "And the plea bargain was a license for Dom Malichera to lie. He had to lie to keep from execution. This dude is the government's star witness! Mr. McDade is a man beset by the fate of being greatly successful in one area of his life while failing in another. His wife's continuous affairs contributed to the nightmare. He's pathetic, talked tough, acted tough, but never followed through." Marty slowed his speech down so the jury could catch up with their notes.

"Alice is pathetic with all her affairs and everybody knows about it. Dom Malichera killed Tom Winters on his own and exploited Raymond McDade. They are both victims, Tom Winters quickly, Raymond McDade slowly. It makes no sense for this successful businessman to pay an evil killer to kill his wife's lover by check. Come place yourself in Dom Malichera's mind to San Quentin prison, the dreariest, most heinous place in California."

Lucas objected, "Irrelevant and also no evidence of that."

"Sustained."

Marty continued in the same vein, "That is the place where they have the gas chamber"

Lucas objected, "Same objection, Your Honor."

"Sustained."

Marty protested, "May it please the Court?"

The judge sustained again. He was impatient to end the trial and get rid of the lawyer.

Marty picked up the pieces. "The deal was to trade the life of Raymond McDade for a murder. The murder which Dom Malichera escaped from by not going to the gas chamber. I know you will find him not guilty. Thanks for your patience."

The court recessed for a fifteen minute break. The jurors were herded outside for the restrooms, telephones at the end of the hall, and water-fountain water. They sat silently on the hallway benches afterward, looking intense, tired, and anxious. The attorneys met with the Judge to review jury instructions again.

Lucas had feelings of doubt from Marty's argument. The defense was trying his best to confuse the jurors, who were all tired and worn out. He began his rebuttal. "Good afternoon. I hope everyone had a good lunch and break, and again, thanks for your patience. I've given rebuttal arguments these past ten years and know how difficult it is for you to sort it all out." He smiled warmly. "Let me tell you a little story. Back in England some time ago, they had regular fox hunts. They would send the fox out into the woods and track them down with horses and hounds. Now, there would always be someone who would follow on foot with fish called red herring. And they would smear the trail of the fox and cause the dogs to lose scent. I mention this story because the defense closing argument is nothing but a red herring to distract you. He is telling you to ignore the evidence, and ignore this and that and all the evidence, except Domingo Malichera. His so-called star witness plea bargained several months after he confessed. He told the truth. He didn't ask for a deal, there were no offers." He went to his table for a glass of water, giving the jury time to digest and think about his statement.

"You are allowed to look at a witness's demeanor. Mr. McDade fakes emotion to create sympathy with you so you would like him and acquit him. Also, what was Dom Malichera, the stone-cold murderer before the defendant got his claws into him? Just a guy going nowhere, but not a criminal. A dealmaker, Dom Malichera? What deal? Life forever in prison? He's not very bright. That's why he's in this mess to begin with. Who's bright? The millionaire businessman. I do agree that he was a failure at being a husband but also a failure at being a murderer. Thank you very much."

The judge dismissed them for the weekend. On Monday the 11th of July, he would give them instructions to decide the verdict. They were again admonished not to discuss the case with anybody at home; that he could have sequestered them to stay under supervision for the weekend. A fitful weekend ensued for all parties.

That Sunday, the prosecution team met for the last time. They drank beer while Mary made batches of Margaritas. She handed them out to the women, and then to the men who drank them like lemonade. They all unwound and relaxed. Mary made her announcement. "Listen everybody. The guy who never gets his picture in the paper, this shy husband of mine, has decided to run for the State Assembly in the next election. The Republican Party approached him." She held up a letter, wrapping her arms proudly around Lucas who blushed.

"Oh, God," Nelson said, "another politician."

"They're as corrupt as some lawyers." Carlson added.

"That's because they're all lawyers." Nelson said.

35

Closure, July 11, 1994

The Honorable Judge Clarke began the day with an hour of jury instruction. The jury filed out to take a controlled break and then deliberate.

Well, this is it, Lucas thought. *If they come back quickly, it would be a conviction. If they take days, then they're arguing, and the time would be on the side of Marty's gang.* The clock ticked. Lucas looked around; saw a newspaper photographer with a reporter in the gallery. Nobody else had hung behind. Lucas left his card with the clerk to call him when the Jury returned. She agreed, after all, the Judge was busy in his chambers and would need to be called, as well.

Lucas went to lunch and returned promptly to his office. He fiddled about with various cases but could not get interested enough to accomplish anything. It was the same when Mary was pregnant the first time. He almost drove himself nuts. At two in the afternoon his secretary received a call, and then appeared in his open doorway. "They want you in the courtroom, Lucas. Three hours deliberation." She held up crossed fingers for good luck as he rushed out the door, briskly walking across the parking lots past the Police Station to the courthouse.

Judge Clarke entered as the Deputy announced his presence, then they all settled down. The room was so quiet that a pin drop could have been heard. "Have you reached a decision?" he asked the jury foreman.

"Yes, we have Your Honor." The foreman handed documents to the Clerk who gave them to the Judge.

"Have the defendant step forward," he said. Raymond McDade was led to the center of the room. The Judge opened the note, read carefully. "Mr. McDade, you have been found guilty of all counts. I will set another date for sentencing. Mr. Tannenbaum, the jury may be dismissed unless you wish to poll them."

A camera flashed as Raymond McDade was led away. "Raymond turned, yelling, "I didn't do it." It was over. Marty Tannenbaum scowled at his assistants, shuffled away. Lucas and Nelson, who also received a call, danced out of the room.

A month after the trial, Domingo Malichera was sentenced to life imprisonment without parole for the murders. His sentence had been delayed until Raymond McDade's trial ended. It had been contingent on his cooperation during the trial. Thus, he avoided the death sentence.

On the morning of Friday, August 26, 1991, a Woodland City Policewoman telephoned Snake at home. His mother answered, "He's not here. He lives on the streets."

"I need my car detailed. Could you call me back on my cell phone if you can arrange it?"

"Okay," Snake's mother answered. "But I can't say when he'll come by."

"Well, that's fine. I'm not in a hurry. I hate taking my car to the carwash. Now, take this number down and don't lose it."

That afternoon the phone rang. Jason would meet her at the house but she needed to bring $100 cash money if she wanted a good job done with paste wax. No credit cards or checks, please.

Later that day Snake wheeled down the street on a bicycle. At the front door of his house he was surprised by Detectives Nelson and Carlson. They hauled him off to the station, in an unmarked car, where he promptly confessed.

An appeal motion for a new trial was promptly filed for Raymond McDade. The new lawyers based their motion on Ray's serious short-term memory problems interfering with his defense. Raymond McDade's sentencing was deferred until the motion was considered.

On Wednesday, November 30, in a crowded courtroom the appeal was bounced. Judge Clarke stated, "Raymond McDade testified for two-and-a-half days, exhibiting a memory that most of us would be envious of."

Later the same day, the attorneys, Raymond McDade, and the Judge met for sentencing. The victims were allowed to speak to the Court. Alice asked for the maximum sentence possible as Ray kept crying, "I didn't do it." Tom Winter's ex-wife asked for restitution to pay for counseling for her younger daughter who had attempted suicide eight times after her father's killing. She was told by the judge that her only recourse was to file a civil suit.

The courtroom continued buzzing with energy until the Judge spoke to Raymond. "Mr. McDade, the Probation Department met with you and reviewed your case for sentencing under their guidelines. They recommend the punishment for Count #1… life imprisonment without the possibility of parole for first-degree murder. Count #2… a sentence of twenty-five years to life for conspiracy to commit murder. Count #3 is six years for first-degree burglary. These crimes were brought on by your jealously and desire to control your wife's relationships. You have no regard for human life and are only interested in having your financial and emotional needs met." There was a gasp from Ray as he covered his face from the flashing cameras of the local newspaper.

"Furthermore," the Judge continued, "this long and exhausting trial bears no fruit. You still maintain total innocence and have no remorse for the victims. You are in a state of denial and feel innocent because you didn't pull the trigger. Your crimes are among the most serious of all and your selfishness offers no excuse or justification."

The courtroom buzzed with everybody talking. The Judge slammed his gavel on the desk. He looked down at Raymond who was mumbling his innocence. "Mr. McDade, you are ordered to pay $10,000 to the Victim's Restitution Fund." He smiled, an event rare on his bench, "But I can credit you for the 1,616 days already served." The galley crowd went ballistic.

Detective Nelson walked past the old courthouse on the way to the station. He stopped, looked up at the Justice chariot with the beautiful Grecian blindfolded female. *Like Moby Dick and Captain Ahab,* he thought, *it beckoned to Ray, "Catch me, and take me down with you into the endless depths of the sea. Into the abyss."*

Inside the cavernous California State Prison in Lancaster, several years later, the morning mail cart stopped by Raymond McDade's windowless cell. The convict left a letter from Walter Davis, the accountant. The letter had already been opened and read by the prison keepers. It began, "Dear Raymond. I am responding to your request for an accounting of the five million dollars in personal assets and the five million dollar radio station sale. There is nothing left. The five years of appeals by George Jackson's extortion resulted in two million dollar attorney's fees to COLA. Then there were the wrongful death and attempted murder suits by the Hispanic boys families. There were the commissions on the sale to your ex-partner and a litany of other expenses over the years.

Alice received almost nothing because all the personal assets were sold for your defense attorneys or encumbered by the same. Maury Rosenfelder, the bankruptcy receiver, succumbed to cancer six months ago, after pursuing five years of successful licensing litigation with the FCC. Fortunately, the final appeal was concluded during his watch on September 5, 1996, when the front man George Jackman and his lawyers lost their last appeal. The COLA assets have all been liquidated and the corporation dissolved."

At that moment a prison control officer watched a clock strike 10 A.M. He picked up a microphone. "Lights out, complements of the California Energy Crisis!" The cells and walkways plunged into darkness. Small emergency lights lit up the hallways. Raymond was left sitting on his bunk in dark solitary confinement, uncontrollably sobbing. 'I need money for my appeal,' he repeated over and over to himself. 'I didn't do it, Dom Malichera did it.'

"Shut the fuck up!" somebody yelled from another cell. Then there was silence.

THE END

About the Author

Phillip Bruce Chute is a businessman–writer. He is currently a tax and financial advisor with a consulting practice in Temecula, California.

Phil served as a paratrooper in the 82nd Airborne Division in the States and in Europe before Vietnam. His ancestry dates back to Warrior-King Robert Bruce of Scotland and the Speaker of Parliament, Chaloner Chute.

As a writer, Phillip has won National and International writing awards for Kiwanis International, His first work, American Independent Business, was a 500-page book published in 1985 and was used as a college text and reference for business entrepreneurs.

Phillip Chute is married to Nenita Lariosa, an educator. Both are semi-retired and work out of their home.